Leadership & Executive Presence:

Inside secrets of strategy, skills, and tactics from corporate officers and coaches

Dr. Jim Kay

Copyright © 2020 Jenna Say Quoi, LLC

All rights reserved. No part of this publication may be reproduced, distributed, or transmitted in any form or by any means, including photocopying, recording, or other electronic or mechanical methods, without the prior written permission of the publisher, except in the case of brief quotations embodied in critical reviews and other noncommercial uses permitted by copyright law.

Dedication:
For Jenna, my wife, who said, "I can't find clear answers on how to develop executive presence."
To my family: ~ May, my oldest daughter, ~ Noah, my only son, ~ Catera, my youngest daughter.

Special Thanks:
Dr. David Rexford and Kathrin Spinnler

Discover other titles by Dr. Jim Kay:

Choices: A story of how personal finance transformed a boy's life with easy steps and inside secrets anyone can follow.

Financial Wellness: Prepare for retirement and the unexpected. Become financially healthy and positively change your life.

Windfall Wisdom: Sudden Wealth, Forever Wealth from specific investment advice and psychological strategies

Fast FIRE: Rules for personal finance to quickly become Financially Independent and Retire Early

Table of Contents

Agreement

Introduction

    Stacy couldn't advance because she didn't have executive presence

        List of traits to improve executive presence:

        Stacy's action steps

        The three main questions Stacy posed

I Leaders are Developed

    Rachel learned how to use the F.B.I. to her advantage

        Rachel's action steps

        Three top take-aways from nurse Rachel

    Two pieces of advice got Brian promoted

        Brian and Julie's action steps

        Three top take-aways from Brian and Julie

    The wrong place and a clear picture got Charley fired

        Charley's action steps

        Learn from Charley's mistakes

    Online videos transformed Billy's life

        Billy's action steps

        Billy's main points

    Nicki's skills as a rocker and a mom gave her executive presence

        Nicki's action steps

        Three top take-aways from rocker, lawyer, and mother: Nicki

    Emma robbed Simon Sinek and it made her a great public speaker

        Emma's action steps

        Three top take-aways from Emma

    Marc wouldn't give Devon a positive recommendation

        Devon's action steps

        Devon's top three

II Get the job done
    Michelle helped young people find their purpose
        Michelle's action steps
        Three top take-aways from Michelle
    Rob carjacked an old lady
        Rob's action steps
        Rob's favorite three take-aways
    Heather lost her job because she solved problems
        Heather's action steps
        Heather's advice
    Chad's unanswered emails solve their own problems
        Chad and Anne's action steps
        The top three take-aways from the coffee shop
    Office politics gave Denzel power, but he had to learn the hard way
        Denzel's action steps
        Three top take-aways from Denzel
III Develop and show your intellect, emotional intelligence, and professional appearance
    Watching Oprah Winfrey helped Oliver move up the corporate ladder
        Oliver's action steps
        Notes from Oliver's executive coach
    Jack hopped on a motorcycle and landed in another high-paying job
        Jack's action steps
        Jack's notes
    Knowing his clients' goals gave Liam a competitive edge
        Liam's action steps
        Liam's top three
    Joyce's night-shift workers do all the labor
        Joyce's action steps
        Joyce's top three

- Mindy created a personal brand that propelled her to the top
  - Mindy's action steps
  - Mindy and Thomas' favorite three
- A dog saved Bethany's life and taught her how to lead
  - Bethany's action steps
  - How to get the best night's sleep
- Ben's formal schooling was online videos and reading in his parents' house
  - Ben's action steps
  - Ben's favored three
- Zach used a ball of Play-Doh to double the company's profits
  - Zach's action steps
  - The top three from Zach
- The advice Phyllis got was worth billions to the company and promotions for her
  - Phyllis' action steps
  - The top three Phyllis would recommend following
- Chuck Norris started a fire in a classroom, and it lit Lou ablaze
  - Lou's action steps
  - Lou's top three

References

Agreement

"Reading a book is a lot like hiring a coach."

Not a lot, no. It's only a little like hiring a coach. For one, you don't get to talk back and forth. I, as your Coach, do the talking. You, the Client, listen and learn. You also save money by buying a book instead of going to a life or executive coach. Most of them are just learning from books as well, so you can keep your cash and kick-start your journey instead. As a free bonus, this coach doesn't keep asking you questions to come up with solutions. The answers you seek are within.

By reading this book, you are entering into an agreement to take the content seriously and apply your new knowledge. You could put the book down, but that would mean backing out of the deal. It's a short manual. Surely you can finish a short book? What if you missed something you needed to know, and it was at the end?

Cost
The cost of this agreement is time and money.

It will take a total of two hours to read this book, but you can't expect growth in this amount of time. You don't live in a movie where you see the main character overcome an obstacle before you finish a tub of popcorn. It will take time for you to change and even longer for people to see your growth.

You'll find different stories, each accompanied by action steps you can take. To get the most out of the book and cut your cost of time:
- ✓ Go through the book's action steps first. Put a mark next to those you already feel you accomplish. Your highlight will give you a sense of triumph before reading the first story. The areas without dots will encourage you to absorb the remaining information by creating a curiosity gap—things you don't know and want to learn.
- ✓ Read one story per night before you turn off your light and go to sleep. After you finish, close your eyes and visualize your ideal life and how you can adopt the strategies you read.
- ✓ Add a nine to the front of the cost of this book. If it was a gift and cost you nothing, picture it costing $90. If it cost you $20, picture it costing $920. When something is a bargain, people don't take it as seriously. When you spend more, it has more value. You're now reading a book of priceless value.

Cancellation Policy

The Client (that's you) may end this agreement at any time with no written notice. Put down the book, and it's over. No hard feelings. However, you did agree to work through the content and gain value from it.

Your recommendation

You had plenty of choices, but you picked this one. If you got something out of it, please recommend it to friends and on social media. Please leave an honest review at the store or online vendor where you bought this book.

Trait Policy

Only try to change one personality trait at a time. Trying to change too much too quickly will slow down your progress. Choose one new behavior change and stick to it each day. Soon, it will become a ritual. A ritual will become a habit. Good habits build the traits you want.

This manual is like a recipe. If you add ALL of the ingredients, you'll have a decadent dessert in which no one wants too much of. Pick the action steps you feel comfortable adding. Choose the ones you need to work on or the ones that will have the most significant impact.

Release of Liability

You can follow a recipe to cook a delicious gourmet meal. You can follow a map to get you where you want to go. You can follow the advice in this book to get a promotion. But like a recipe, don't blame the text for your problems.

The Coach (that's the author) makes no guarantees, representations, or warranties of the materials within this book. The Coach will NOT be liable to the Client for any damages. The Client is aware that coaching is in no way psychological counseling or medical advice. You understand and acknowledge that you will NOT agree with or appreciate some of the material written in this book. The Coach will not be legally liable for the actions the Client may or may not undertake as a result of following the advice in this book. No responsibility is made or given, and the Client reading such information agrees not to hold the author responsible or liable in any form or fashion, for such actions taken of their own accord.

The Client agrees that using any of the advice in this book is at their own risk. Books are provided "as is," without warranty, possibly a few spelling mistakes, and grammatical errors. The Client chooses to read this book and takes full responsibility for the decisions they make as well as the consequences. The Client enters into this agreement with the thorough understanding they are responsible for creating results.

Introduction

Look at yourself from an outside perspective. Do you see a leader? Do you have executive presence? Do you possess the courage to take calculated risks to advance your organization? Learn what it takes to become a leader and show executive presence.

Stacy couldn't advance because she didn't have executive presence

Stacy's smart heels clicked as she led me into her light and airy corner office on the fiftieth floor of the glass office building.

"Please, take a seat," she said, offering me a glass of water. "Now. What can I help you with?"

"As you know from my letter, my name is Jim. I'm interviewing executives who are the best at specific aspects of leadership and executive presence." I cleared my throat and opened my leather-bound journal. I then continued, "I talk with a lot of different people and get their impressions of who could give the best advice for rising officers. Your name came up a few times from different networking events."

Stacy gave a superiority smile. She then said, "Thank you. It's flattering to learn my colleagues, and I guess even people outside my field think highly of me."

"They do," I responded. "I travel around and interview people who can give a narrow-focused light on the executive presence traits and leadership tools they found to be most useful. I take notes." I held up my journal and a basic fountain pen. "I use what these leaders say to formulate action steps for those who are climbing the corporate ladder. Sometimes these leaders say things they are doing and don't even realize how it impacts their executive presence. I use my outside perspective. I pull the information, form it into a shiny pearl, and deliver it to the reader. I want to write a coaching manual that is short, concise, and shoots from the hip. I feel people need easy-to-follow answers to otherwise vague directions."

"Well, I'd love to help." Stacy smiled at me. "As you know, I'm the Chief Operations Officer of a Fortune 500 company now. But merely showing up for work each day didn't get me here. In fact, at 23 years old, I felt like a complete failure. I had graduated with an MBA in Leadership from Stanford. The school's learning labs gave me useful experience. I had more knowledge than managers who had been with the company for years. But when I spoke to my supervisor about getting a promotion, it felt like everything I had done was for nothing."

Stacy pointed out the New York office building window. I could see where she was directing my attention, another skyscraper within view. "That is the company where I used to work. I had just completed a big project that made them a ton of money. A few days later, I scheduled a meeting with my supervisor. I told him I wanted to get honest feedback on how the project went. The conversation itself went fine until I asked about advancement in the company." Stacy's eyes looked stoic and mad. "He told me I lacked executive presence."

Stacy looked back toward the old office and her lower jaw set firm. Then, she continued: "I didn't go through all that school, then work night and day for someone to tell me I couldn't advance because I lacked executive presence. At first, I was angry. I was in denial—figuring he needed an excuse not to promote me. The next morning, I was in the shower thinking over the conversation, and a little part of me thought: 'He's right. The degree and experience didn't give me an executive presence. I had to learn what it took to climb the corporate ladder.' I had professors out West teach me about business. I needed someone to train me in how to act, talk, and what to look like." She moved away from the window and back toward her desk.

"The next day, I hired a coach," Stacy continued. "I got some recommendations and interviewed a few. I found one who would talk with me in person during lunch."

Stacy shook her head. "Don't ask me how much I spent on that coach."

"It was a lot?" I asked.

"You could say that! $6,200, but it was all worth it."

Stacy wrote a name on a piece of paper and slid it across her mahogany desk. "This is the coach I used." She directed me to come back to the window.

She pointed down to the sidewalk, where we could see the umbrella of a hotdog vendor. "The first meeting we had was very casual. We sat on that bench, eating hotdogs. The coach asked me to come up with stories about some of the people walking by. As we sat eating, I was to make assumptions about each person like where they work, how they act."

Stacy took a drink of water and continued, "I wish I could remember all the questions I had to answer about the people. The ones I remember were: Are they polite? Do they get the job done? Do they meet deadlines and give their best work? Do coworkers like them? Do they have self-confidence? When they talk, are they concise, direct, and simple?"

Stacy brushed some invisible lint off her blazer. "Observing the passers-by helped me to notice traits that made a person appear more authoritative. The same week, I found a female senior vice-president in our company to emulate. This CIO had an executive presence. I first noticed her one day in the break room. People usually finish the coffee pot or leave less than a cup at the bottom for the next person to struggle to make more. I came into the break room and saw her making the coffee. I was a bit surprised. She was an executive, and here she was caring for her team enough to make the next brew.

'I caught you,' I yelled. 'You're the one making the strong stuff.'

She grabbed some coffee grounds and tossed them in the air like a magician disappearing in a cloud of smoke. By the time the coffee fell to the ground, she was out of the door. That was the day I decided I would model myself after her but add my own brand. Notice I always wear a splash of red?"

She let her fingertips rub against her bright blouse. "That alone wasn't enough to advance my career. But looking at how other people perceive me made me realize I always need to look and act for the job I want. I'm not saying to go overboard. A junior executive shouldn't dress like the CEO because he wants that job. He needs to have a consistent, tailored, clean look about himself. One afternoon on a bench, eating hotdogs gave me a perception change that had the most impact."

After Stacy and I spoke, I looked up the coach. He agreed to give me the list of traits he discusses with his clients to help them improve their executive presence.

List of traits to improve executive presence:

- ✓ Shows up to work on time.
- ✓ Polite to people.
- ✓ Does their best work.
- ✓ Takes the initiative, doing things for the company, not asked.
- ✓ Meets deadlines.
- ✓ Avoids gossip.
- ✓ Avoids abusing company time (playing computer games at work, on social media, shopping).
- ✓ Takes personal responsibility for mistakes.
- ✓ Good at their job.
- ✓ Liked by coworkers.
- ✓ Self-confident.
- ✓ Good at using eye-contact.
- ✓ Avoids the use of profanity.

- ✓ Avoids slang.
- ✓ Avoids off-colored or rude jokes.
- ✓ Has gratitude.
- ✓ Concise when delivering a message.
- ✓ Has a sense of humor.
- ✓ Gets the job done.

Stacy's action steps

- ✓ Ask for feedback from your peers and supervisor.
- ✓ Be polite and friendly with coworkers.
- ✓ Get the job done by providing error-free work.
- ✓ Meet your deadlines.
- ✓ Show your self-confidence.
- ✓ Communicate in a concise, direct, and straightforward manner.
- ✓ Use someone to emulate, but add your own flair.
- ✓ Act and dress for the position you want.
- ✓ View yourself from an outside perspective and make the necessary changes.

The three main questions Stacy posed

How would a stranger view you?

What authoritative traits do you have, and which ones do you need?

Do you wear clothing that is flattering to your body shape, clean, and projects the image you want people to remember?

I
Leaders are Developed

Leadership is simple. You don't need complicated methods or theories. Leaders have been effectively making progress with employees for thousands of years. The best leaders, throughout history, have incorporated three ingredients for success:
- Personal wellbeing—fitness. If a leader is sick, tired, or dead, they can't make the best decisions.
- Interact with all levels of employees in a genuine, caring way.
- The proper set up and running of your team.

Rachel learned how to use the F.B.I. to her advantage

"Jim, thanks for meeting me. I know I'm not one of your typical interviews. When I heard about what you were doing, I had to reach out." Rachel was a nurse and had worked with many doctors and in a few different hospitals. "I've come to realize what is good leadership and poor."

"I'm thankful you're willing to give up some of your time to talk," I responded. We sat in the cafeteria of a large hospital. We were on the ground floor. Just outside the windows were also areas to sit among the landscaping. "On the phone, you mentioned two types of leaders, those who use fear and those who don't."

Rachel took a drink of coffee from a white mug. "I was new to nursing and working under this doctor. He was in his early thirties, and I was in my early twenties. He wasn't a leader but a boss. Anytime I would speak up about the diagnosis, he would shut me down. It even made me feel bad about my lack of education compared to his. I'm not saying I was always right. But I know for certain he made some bad decisions. Some of his patients died because he didn't listen to me. I shouldn't admit this, but some of his patients died because I didn't speak up."

"Rachel, you must feel terrible," I responded.

"I do. I also learned you have to forgive yourself and others and move on. You can't live your life hating people for mistakes they've done in the past. We all make mistakes. I would be a miserable old nurse if I never let things from the past go." Rachel wasn't old, probably mid-forties. A touch of grey coming through her blonde hair.

"How long did you stay with Doctor Death?"

Rachel smiled, "Not long. After him, I worked with another doctor. She was older and cared for everyone. At first, I was scared to speak up. I lived in fear from the previous doctor that my opinion wouldn't matter." Rachel paused and drank some coffee. "This doctor kept asking my thoughts as we examined patients. Finally, I spoke up. She removed the fear by having open discussions."

"It sounds like even if you gave a wrong answer, the doctor would still show her appreciation."

"Exactly right, Jim." Rachel beamed because someone finally understood her.

"She was a great doctor. I owe her a lot. She even recommended me for a promotion. There was an opening for an executive assistant to the CEO of the hospital. The pay wasn't much better than I was making as a nurse, but I would be able to give back in a new way."

"Did you take the job?" I asked.

"I did, and I learned the importance of managing by wandering around." Rachel paused and watched me write some notes in my journal. "The CEO instilled values in the employees by showing how to act. He cared for the patients. He would pick up trash. He would wipe down door handles."

I nodded my head, "That's great."

Rachel continued, "Above anything else, The CEO listened to employees' concerns. He talked with every level of employee and cared about what they were saying. I would walk with him, and he would explain why some problems couldn't be solved and how he would work on others." Rachel stopped talking as someone came to the table and refilled our coffees.

We thanked the waiter, and Rachel continued, "The CEO taught me a technique to get people on your side. I even witnessed him use it. He called it the F.B.I. but it wasn't about spies or law enforcement. When you face a problem, you explain how the situation made you feel. That's the F. You connect those feelings with the behavior the person is showing. There's your B. The last part is your intentions. What do you need to change."

"It sounds like the order doesn't even matter," I said.

"No, the order can change based on how you want to present the issues. For example, we would walk around talking with employees. One employee would always complain about his pay. At first, the CEO would explain the pay structure and how it was fair. On the third time the same employee complained about his pay, the CEO used the F.B.I. approach. It was something like: 'I feel you aren't valued here as an employee and want more money to feel like your efforts have worth. But you don't do anything for yourself to advance your career. We offer training and promotions here at the hospital. If your salary is to improve, you need to take it upon yourself to advance.'"

I smiled as I heard each of the letters used. "I could hear each part: feeling, behavior, and intentions. I could also hear how that would work to bring about change. Either the employee gets more training or shuts up about his income."

Rachel chuckled a bit at my harsh response. "The CEO taught me something else. There are three types of people in the world. Most are good and care about one another, like the employee who wanted more money. Then some want to sue the hospital. The F.B.I. method won't work with those people. Let the lawyers handle them. The CEO would refuse to talk with those who were litigious. The final group was just plain evil. We would break ties with them. Not communicate at all. He wouldn't respond to them and wouldn't let any of us respond either. We didn't come across many people like this, but a few patients would fit into this category each year."

"In interviewing people like you, I don't come across many people who are trying to sue or are evil. I did have one interview, and the guy was a bit spiteful."

Rachel tapped the table. "I don't want to take up any more of your time, but I do have one more story about getting ideas and people involved in discussions."

"Great, let's hear it."

"The same CEO I was working for had to cut costs one year. He asked every employee to write down 15 ideas on how to reduce expenses. I was on the team who had to go through the suggestions. The first five were all the same from everyone. But after those, people started to get creative. We ended up taking a lot of suggestions. And because they came from the employees, they were on board too. It wasn't just management saying to stop waste."

"Rachel, this has been a great time. The coffee isn't bad here, either." I closed my journal and stood up. "I appreciate your candid talk and glad we met to learn about what makes great leadership."

Rachel's action steps

- ✓ Engage with every level of employee.
- ✓ Manage by wandering around.
- ✓ Instill values by showcasing how to act.
- ✓ Listen and respond to employee concerns.
- ✓ Gather and use horizontal communication to share ideas.
- ✓ Get 15 anonymous ideas—duplicates are gone after the first five, and those who aren't comfortable sharing feel safe by keeping their name off the suggestion.
- ✓ Don't use fear to keep people quiet.
- ✓ Remove fear and let people know failure is a learning opportunity—discuss cooperatively what went wrong.
- ✓ If someone gives a wrong answer, still show appreciation.
- ✓ When correcting behavior, share your feelings based on their behavior and tell them what you need—your intentions.
- ✓ Let lawyers talk with those who want to sue and don't engage with those you suspect are out to cause pain.
- ✓ To make changes and adaptations quickly, talk with workers at the bottom—they are first to notice when modifications are needed.

Three top take-aways from nurse Rachel

Learn how to talk with people and listen to those people on the front lines.
- ༶ Talk to all levels of employees to find out what needs to change in the organization.
- ༶ Share how their behavior makes you feel and what needs to be changed.
- ༶ Remove fear by showing appreciation for people's candid responses.

Ask for many ideas to get people to start thinking creatively and beyond the basics.

Showcase your values by wandering around and interacting with employees and customers.

Two pieces of advice got Brian promoted

"Before my sponsor, Julie, comes to meet with us, let me tell you how two things I learned in high school got me a six-figure salary."

Brian looked around furtively and hushed, to signal that he was confessing a secret. "I had an executive presence. I could get the job done with confidence and poise. I always kept my cool under pressure. When someone tried to make me angry or stressed, I could remain calm and friendly. I owe that to a breathing technique I learned while in high school: 4 7 8 (Weil, 2020). Here do it with me. Silently, breathe in through your nose for four seconds—fill your lungs."

Brian put his hand on his chest and inhaled, watching me as I copied him.

"Hold it for seven seconds. Exhale through your mouth for a slow eight seconds. Control the breath by pursing your lips together." Brian made a whooshing noise as he exhaled.

"I use this when unfortunate events happen," he continued. "It's how you react that matters. I used the 4 7 8 breathing technique when things didn't go well." Brian repeated the exercise a few more times.

He tapped his head. "Remember how I said I learned this in high school? That's because I had all these false conceptions. I thought people were talking bad about me. I always worried about what people thought about me, how I dressed, what I said. These false conceptions drove me crazy. I met with a counselor my mom found. She taught me the technique and told me, 'You can only control your response.' Those two things transformed and saved my life."

Brian continued, "Do you want to hear how the counselor's wisdom saved my life?" I nodded and sat up in my chair.

"I was still in high school. We lived in the inner city of Arlington, Virginia. Every morning, I walked to school and back as it was only a few blocks from our tiny apartment. I was the new kid. Four high schools in four years—I was always the new kid. I was also overweight. Fat." Brian puffed out his cheeks and signaled with his arms how big he was.

"I was walking home from school, and three kids a bit older than me stopped me and pulled a knife. I can still see that knife in my memory. I can still hear them yelling at me in a foreign language. My training kicked in, not my ninja skills, but what the counselor taught me. 'You can only control your reaction.' I breathed in for a slow four seconds. I held that breath for seven seconds. I released it for eight seconds. Then, I looked at the three kids and the knife. I figured I couldn't outrun them, and as a fat kid, I used all my money buying honey buns from the vending machine, which meant I couldn't even bribe them. They didn't speak English, so I turned and strolled away. Their shouts faded behind me as I kept walking."

Brian went over to the door, opened it, and looked down the hall. "Great, Julie isn't here yet; let's fast forward away from high school to that first high-paying job. I had learned a valuable thought pattern in high school. Along with the breathing exercises, I realized I couldn't control events or other people. I can only control my reaction. This thought pattern, along with the breathing technique, are what propelled me to the high-paying job. My calm attitude showcased my self-control.

My superiors saw I could control my reaction and dismiss what other people thought. Because of my level head, I earned senior level opportunities. Knowing how to breathe, I showed people I had emotional stability to lead a team."

He paused and wrinkled his forehead.

"What is it, Brian?" I asked.

"I have someone you might want to talk with. After we meet, do you want to interview someone who might have an executive presence on the surface but lacks couth?"

"You seem cultured and refined. Sure, I'd like to meet the opposite of you." I responded.

There was a knock on the door, and we turned in our chairs to face it as it swung open.

An elegantly dressed, tall lady slid through the door. Her brown hair pulled tight in a bun. We both stood as she walked toward us. She shook my hand and said, "Good morning. Sorry, I'm late. A meeting ran long. I'm Julie, Brian's sponsor, and mentor. My goal is to groom him for a position like mine." Julie sat down in the chair next to me. Brain moved behind his desk.

"So, what have you discussed so far?" Julie asked.

I shifted in my chair uncomfortably, waiting for Brian to speak. He allowed for a lengthy pause. I heard a faint whooshing as he exhaled, signaling he was using his breathing technique.

"We were talking about my old job and how I didn't have all the tools I needed to display executive presence," he said.

Julie smiled. "Brian is smart, and he's a quick learner. This guy just needs to work on a few more things. For one, he needs to lose the ego and have some cheerful interactions to bring up colleagues during meetings. He comes across as too superior. To control the room, you need to let other people shine. Let them know, 'What can I do for you?' This is more important than 'How will you help me?' Brian also needs to work on forgiveness. He doesn't come out and say it, but after someone makes a mistake, he'll give these little looks before a project is assigned. Employees pick up on that, and it kills company morale. People learn from their mistakes and deserve a second chance." Julie paused and looked at both of us. "Do you have time for a story?"

"Sure, we have all the time you need," I responded.

Julie sat up in her chair, eager to pass along wisdom. "Years ago, before Brian joined us, a guy named Kevin was leading a huge project. It was a $10 million deal. He screwed up. He failed to look at all the possible pitfalls and didn't prepare for the worst-case scenario. He should have thought about all the ways this deal could have gone side-ways and how he would deal with each problem, but he didn't. The deal cost the company $10 million." Julie sat back in her chair to allow the gravity of the situation to sink in. "Kevin got called into the CEO's office. He was terrified, thinking that was going to be his last day. But the CEO just said: 'I've invested $10 million in your education. I plan on keeping you around for quite a while. Now go out there, find another deal, and learn from your mistake.'"

Brian spoke up. "That's just like him. I'm glad I work at a company that gives me the confidence mistakes are forgiven."

Julie stood up and walked to the back of her chair. "Do you want to hear another story?" She asked. "I have a boxer friend. We grew up together. I've given him some advice from time to time. Not about boxing but about how to show courage. This boxer's problem was energy management. He would work out with weights in the morning, then go for a run. When he got back, he did jump rope and speed drills. By 9:00 AM, he was out of energy and couldn't do much else. He also had a day-job, but sucked-wind for the rest of the day and ate all day to try to regain his momentum. He was a good looking guy, and those types do well in pharmaceutical sales, so they kept him around. But his energy management was so bad, I bought him a shirt that read, 'How to talk to me in the mid-afternoon? Don't.'"

Julie paused as we chuckled. "One day, he was working out in the morning, and a trainer came up to him. The trainer told him he was pretty good and suggested he sparred with a boxer who's coming in that afternoon. The compliment got to his head. He checked his schedule and realized he could swing in after his last appointment. When he arrived at 3:00 PM, his sparring partner was the female lightweight champion for boxing. Of course, he put up the mandatory, 'I've never hit a lady before,' argument. By 3:20, they were sparring, and at 3:40, my buddy had peed in his pants and all over the rink. The female champ had accidentally hit him in the bladder. My guy hadn't gone to the bathroom since before his last sales meeting. It was a hard hit and a lot of pee—a mop wasn't enough."

I quickly stifled my snort as Brian said, "That's a funny story, but what about the advice you gave him?"

Julie nodded and responded, "A boxer has courage. He knows he can fight because he's practiced. Uncomfortable situations are practice for the tougher challenges. My buddy may have pissed himself and lost the bout, but he learned from his mistake: when you get a chance, go to the toilet. I didn't have to teach him that. A 135-pound female did it for me."

After a pause, Julie continued. "The most important lesson for him was: 'Know what you want and ask for what you want.' Be decisive—even if you're not entirely certain yet. Make a decision and stick with it. I also helped my buddy to realize the cost of not following through. He wanted to be this great boxer, but he didn't calendarize any goals. He needed to go after what he wanted and ask for it. He had a goal of getting paid to fight but solely hoped for discovery. It doesn't happen that way. Put on the calendar when you want it to happen, take steps to train, and get to the level people would pay to watch you fight. Not a street fight on social media but an organized match."

Brian and Julie's action steps

- ✓ Get the job done with confidence, on time, with poise, while keeping your cool.
- ✓ Act calm, self-assured, in control. Don't appear nervous.
- ✓ Don't act rashly. Use the 4 7 8 breathing technique before reacting.
- ✓ Always display your emotional stability and ability to lead a team. Opportunities will start to appear.
- ✓ Focus on what you can control.
- ✓ Control your response, and don't let false conceptions drive you crazy.
- ✓ Practice self-control—you can't control events, only your reaction.
- ✓ Have cheerful interactions to bring up colleagues.
- ✓ Always enter conversations with the thought of: "What can I do for you?"
- ✓ Control your energy management.

Three top take-aways from Brian and Julie

To earn senior level opportunities.
- ↣ Control your reaction.
- ↣ Keep a level head.
- ↣ Use the 4 7 8 breathing technique during stressful times.

While you're working through your senior-level opportunities.
- ↣ Let other people shine.
- ↣ Have good-natured fun.
- ↣ Make the meetings enjoyable.

To make the most of your senior-level opportunities.

- Put yourself in uncomfortable situations to practice for the tougher challenges.
- Be decisive.
- Calendarize your goals.

The wrong place and a clear picture got Charley fired

After my interview with Brian, he walked me down to Charley's office. The office was a few floors down. Brian introduced us, "Charley, this is Jim. He's interviewing people for a book on executive presence and leadership. I thought about who has EP here in the building, and your name was at the bottom of my list." Charley laughed at the jab.

Charley spoke up, "Nice one Brian. I guess you want me to tell him some of my stories." Brian nodded, said his goodbyes, and walked out the door.

I sat down. "Charley, I heard you might have some stories of what an executive should not do to move up the corporate ladder."

"I haven't made it as high as Brian, but I'm doing alright for myself," Charley stated. "Unfortunately, there was one thing I lacked that kept me from advancing as quickly as my counter-parts: my team's trust. Talking without care for other people's feelings does not show executive presence. Connection, cooperation, and humility are what executives need to display. Those things build rapport and trust, but I didn't realize this until it was too late. I would tell insensitive jokes, the ones that made me look like a bigot. The day I was fired, I found out people refused to work with me because of those off-handed comments. Everyone in my office thought I was a bully."

I tilted my head and started to speak. "But . . ."

Charley shook his head. "I know. You thought bullying only happened in school. Not true. Even Fortune 500 companies have executives who are bullies. I made fun of how people dressed, and I played these practical jokes. One day, I thought it would be hilarious if I replaced all of the graphs in someone's sales presentation with photos from his family. It was funny but the wrong thing to do in a business situation."

Charley laughed to himself, checked his watch, and said, "Here's another joke, I thought, was hilarious. It was at the aquarium."

Charley pointed south and continued. "We were there on a company retreat. Our company isn't huge, so other guests were there too. For the first hour, we met in a large conference room, and then for a break, we walked around the aquarium in small groups. There was a family that kept up with my small group. They kept getting in our way. The grandfather was in a wheelchair, and he never had a good view of the fish because the family would push him to the side and then get in his way. The grandkids would ignore everything their parents said, and the whole family ignored the man in the wheelchair. They pushed him from one tank to the next exhibit, giving him the worst view. I had been to the aquarium before. I knew at the end of this long corridor was an amazing display of saltwater fish with coral and waves. As the family bickered with one another, I took the old man and wheeled him away. No one in the family saw it. I pushed him right up to the glass of the beautiful fish. I stood with him until I heard the family start to yell, 'Poppi, Poppi!' then I walked away. In a way, it was nice. At the same time, I was a jackass.

The small group I was with from my company thought it was funny. They told others in the company, and it didn't translate well. In hindsight, I was an ass. I still wonder what the family thought. 'How did Poppi get down here?'"

Charley paused and sighed. "Well, for the most part, I had respect and looked the part until it all came crashing down within one week. At this point, everyone knows the entire story about my sexual inappropriateness. Since then, I've come a long way. I was shallow and distant. Like I lived in a bubble, and it only got worse as time passed. The week before I got fired, I walked into a meeting late. I saw everyone looking depressed. In a sarcastic tone, I asked, 'Who died?' Sure enough, the senior vice-president's mom had died the night before. There he was, sitting in the meeting, glaring at me."

Charley muted his cell phone after the third notification. "But those incidents alone didn't get me fired. Someone took a picture of me in a compromising position with one of my subordinates. The photo was clearer than you could imagine. The boss called it 'a sexual misconduct scandal in a corporate environment,' and it could and did get me fired. I tried to lie and cover it up, but those lies did more damage than help. I realize now, when you mess up, confess up. Take the blame for your mistakes, and move forward. I didn't do that either."

Charley looked at me, sheepishly. "Do you want to hear what I did after getting fired?" he asked, and I nodded enthusiastically. "No one told security of my termination, so that night, I went back into the office with nine cans of tuna. I went into each office, took down the curtain rod, and shoved it full of tuna. Oh, the stench must have been horrific."

Charley's action steps

- ✓ Be conscious of how you make people feel as they work with you.
- ✓ Display connection, cooperation, and humility to build trust.
- ✓ Learn from your mistakes.
- ✓ Don't lie.
- ✓ Don't retaliate or get revenge.
- ✓ Don't participate in a cover-up.
- ✓ Don't bully.
- ✓ Don't tell insensitive jokes.
- ✓ Use good manners.
- ✓ Avoid all sexual impropriety.
- ✓ Display your integrity with pride: Your character is your best calling card.

Learn from Charley's mistakes

Earn trust.
- ௸ Build connections.
- ௸ Showcase your cooperation.
- ௸ Have humility.

Show your people skills.
- ௸ Don't come across as shallow.
- ௸ Don't try to be funny at other people's expense.
- ௸ Keep your romantic relationships with people outside the office.

Take the high-ground when you've slipped up.
- ௸ Don't try to get revenge.
- ௸ Don't cover-up mistakes.
- ௸ Don't lie. Be candid.

Online videos transformed Billy's life

"I attribute my success to watching YouTube videos." Billy laughed. He moved his muscular arms in circles, pointing out the expensive decorations in his large office. Billy's voice changed. In a slurred country dialect, he continued, "I grew up in West Virginia, a coal miner's son. We all talked like this—a little too high-pitched with a twang. Life was very different back then. For example, I always used to ride in my dad's messy pickup truck. I loved rummaging around in the glove compartment. You could find all kinds of treasures. But one day, I decided to reach under the seat, where I felt something hard and cold. I pulled it out, and my heart stopped. It was a pistol. My hands trembled as I held it up to the light. "Dad?" I asked. "Do you . . . do you use this?" He glanced over, unperturbed. 'Seldom do.' For years I thought he said 'sold 'em to.' I thought he sold guns on the side."

"Wow," I said. "That's crazy!"

Billy's voice changed, and the dialect was gone. "I wasn't like my dad—I knew I didn't want to be in the coal industry or carry a loaded gun under a seat. I started my working career in a warehouse and saved my money for college. Luckily, I also got a government grant, so I didn't have to go into debt."

Billy signaled with his hand that he was skipping forward in time. "In college, people made fun of me. It soon turned into full-blown bullying. They called me a dumb hick, a cracker, and even a coal lump. It took me three months to make a friend. One guy down the hall didn't make fun of me. He never bullied me and even stood up for me in front of the others." Billy pointed to the office next to his. "Tom was the only one who treated me with respect. That's why he's in the position he's in now, making six figures."

Billy turned to his computer, and I sat looking out of the window at the glass building next door. It was so close that I could see the harried employees in the open-plan office, flitting back and forth. I looked back at Billy's calm, cool office. What a contrast! "I asked Tom to come over. He can explain it better than me," Billy interrupted my thoughts. "I owe my success to him. Tom helped me overcome the things I was lacking, like my poor, coarse dialect, and grammar. He suggested I watch public speakers on YouTube, listening to their pronunciation, and proper grammar. He also corrected how I spoke. When I said something with a twang, he would say it the right way, and I practiced with him."

There was a knock on the door, and a sandy-haired man stuck his head in. "Hey Billy, what's . . . Oh sorry. I didn't know you had someone here." Tom was tall, well-groomed, polished. He looked the part of an executive.

Billy introduced us, and I explained how he'd told me about his phoenix-like transformation from a stereo-typical West Virginian to a gentleman within two years. Tom nodded. "I can tell you I saw real improvement. Billy here used his time to listen to motivational speakers. He changed his dialect. Kind of like how someone who watches a bunch of British television can fake a British accent. By our junior year, Billy could turn on and off his West Virginia dialect." Tom tried to fake a country voice, but it sounded like a Red-Dirt song.

"Billy became one of the best public speakers on campus. He was concise and compelling with his straight talk. He kept things simple and humorous. These elements made him seem like he had self-confidence."

Tom smiled at Billy, who nodded.

"I realized a few things from watching those professional speakers," Billy said. "They kept their main point to less than ten words and used silence after those compelling words. Not too much but enough to let the important points sink in. Another thing I noticed was how and when they moved around the room. The best speakers usually made a total of three main points. Before they began their first topic, they made eye contact, stood still, and said their headline. They would expound on that one headline. Then, they strode over to another part of the room, stopped, and made eye contact. Then they said the next headline. In small group meetings, some even used people's names."

Tom walked closer to his boss and asked, "Can I tell him about the girl on drugs?" Billy nodded.

"Billy and I were at a dinner party, and there must have been 20 - 30 people there. It was a great big house in the suburbs, a beautiful place. At about 9:00 PM, four teenagers came in, trying to avoid us and slip upstairs. The host spotted them and called: 'Come down here and introduce yourselves.' One of the girls came back with her friends behind her. She introduced herself and her friends. The host told them to get food from the kitchen, and they made a bee-line for it. About an hour and a half later, the dinner-party guests started to leave. Billy and I had come to the party together, and I gave him the signal we should head out—we have codes for those things. Billy signaled we should stay, so we stayed to help clean the dishes while everyone else left." Tom paused and looked at his boss as he was nodding.

"Billy took aside the host to talk to her in private. I couldn't help overhearing the conversation as I washed the dishes in the kitchen. 'Your daughter is doing drugs,' Billy told her. There was a long silence, and time seemed to stop. I felt like I was floating in space, waiting for the conversation to continue. Why would he say something like that? Finally, she spoke up. 'There's no possible way my daughter could be doing something so foolish.' But Billy couldn't be deterred. With even more conviction, he repeated, 'I'm certain your daughter is doing drugs.' She called her daughter down and confronted her. Of course, the teenager denied it. Billy kept to his guns. 'Can't you admit to your mom you're doing drugs? Tell her the last time you tried something.' The young girl insisted once again she was clean."

Tom stopped, and Billy picked up the story from there. "I knew the girl was a drug user and couldn't leave the situation without making certain her mom knew the truth. Half an hour later, the teenager still hadn't confessed, and so we took off, leaving a fuming family behind. I didn't hear from that mom for six months, and the friendship seemed over. Until one day, she and the daughter showed up here at this office. They wanted to tell me I saved the young girl's life. It turns out, her mother got her tested the day after the party, and she was using drugs just as I'd said. She immediately got her treatment in Colorado. Part of the healing was for the teen to break-off her old friendships. Even the teen told me, 'Thanks. You did the right thing.'" Billy paused for a moment like his next line was going to be imperative. "I live by my values. I used my direct, no-nonsense communication style to make my point known."

Tom's eyes were welling up. We both looked at him, and he changed the subject. "When Billy first came to college, his voice was too high-pitched. Have you ever seen an executive with a high-pitched voice? No—they don't exist. People either learn to lower their inflections, or they don't make it to senior-level positions. I told him to watch some videos of voice coaches."

"Yeah, my voice was too high. It wasn't easy to change that, especially because I got teased about my language exercises. One day, my roommate came in while I was Ba Ba Baing." Billy was almost singing. "I just ignored them. Future success was more important than the bullies. I learned two things by watching voice trainers. Use your diaphragm and close your vocal cords for a deeper louder voice." Billy started to sing nonsense sounds.

"That's how he practiced every day," Tom said as I chuckled.

"The best presenters didn't rely on notes, slides, or devices," Billy explained. "They also never used diminishing words—um, like, kind-of, so, right, ah, sort-of, and you-know. By my junior year in college, I was the star-student in public speaking. I leveraged that ability to climb the corporate ladder."

"Yeah, and Billy always kept me by his side. Each move he made, I followed him within the year. He jumped from place to place, getting the best new opportunity and salary, and each time, he found an opportunity for me. Billy, I don't know if I ever said this. Thanks. I appreciate the chance to move up with you."

Billy pretended to wipe a tear from his eye, stood up, and gave Tom a bro-hug. "We are allies, friends, and we owe each other a lot."

Billy's action steps

- ✓ Minimize a strong dialect.
- ✓ Learn to write and speak with correct grammar.
- ✓ Pronounce words correctly.
- ✓ Train to become a public speaker.
- ✓ Use concise and compelling language.
- ✓ Keep your main point to ten words or less.
- ✓ When speaking, stay silent for several seconds after delivering your main point.

- ✓ Keep your communication simple.
- ✓ Add in a sense of humor or funny stories.
- ✓ When presenting, stand still, make a point, then move to another part of the room, looking at other people. Make a new point, and repeat the process.
- ✓ Don't rely on notes, slides, or devices.
- ✓ Don't use filler words—a pause is more acceptable.
- ✓ Use people's names to keep their attention.
- ✓ Train your voice like a singer to keep it low, controlled, and projecting.
- ✓ Be appreciative of people helping to advance your career by helping them out in return.

Billy's main points

Make friends.
- ಙ Stand up for people, even when they're not looking.
- ಙ Let friends know your appreciation.
- ಙ With your words and actions, make people feel valued and liked.

Polish how you come across to others.
- ಙ Lose the harsh dialect.
- ಙ Control and reduce high-pitched speaking.
- ಙ Become a dynamic public speaker.
- ಙ Pronounce words correctly.
- ಙ Use acceptable grammar.
- ಙ Your language needs to be concise and compelling.

Live by your values.
- ಙ Take a values test and write out the ones important to you.
- ಙ One of your values needs to be honesty. You won't go far when people don't think you have integrity.
- ಙ Your organization also needs to hold high values.

Nicki's skills as a rocker and a mom gave her executive presence

"What was the one experience that gave me today's success? My first career—if you can call those three years of eating dirt a career. I started my working life as a rocker. We never made it big. No one remembers me. Have you ever heard of my stage-name of Nicki Sain?" I shook my head, no. "I didn't think so. We toured and had a manager who tried to help, but we were atrocious. What I got out of those three years was stage-presence.

Before I stood in front of a microphone, I was a skinny, meek, mouse-haired girl. Performing taught me to use my body language to match the mood, tone, and lyrics of the songs. Instead of looking like my 120-pound frame, I would have power poses—making myself look bigger by standing tall and puffing out my chest. This mild-mannered girl acted the part. I learned to read the crowd and change up the order of the songs. Even my eye-contact excited the audience."

Nicki paused, smiled, and looked up. I could still see the rocker in her stylish, short brown hair and sparkly eyes. "My manager started to set up interviews," she continued. "He told me, 'Don't slump or look small. Your body language needs to express how you want yourself, and this band portrayed—powerful.' During every interview, I was as loud as my songs. I didn't hesitate when I talked. I came across confident."

Nicki stood and looked out the window of her home office. Her manicured lawn, typical for the suburbs of Chicago, was dotted with ornamental bushes and a koi pond. She tapped the window and said, "My second career taught me another vital lesson. I became a mother and started telling my daughter bedside stories each night. She insisted I tell her true stories. I would embellish and change the experience to get the point across—most of my adventures aren't appropriate for six-year-old ears. I never told her the point of the story directly, but we discussed the take-away together so that she figured it out for herself. During my story-telling career, I learned humor was important. Weeks after I told my little girl a story, she remembered it, especially the funny parts. I always created an engaging title, almost over-blown, and set the scene and characters. Each story had a conflict and demonstrated how the main character overcame that obstacle. The problem could be a bad guy, a terrible situation, or even an internal conflict. Those stories, together with a heck of a lot of schooling and my performance skills, brought about my third career."

Nicki moved back to her desk, sat, and pointed to a law degree on the wall. "I became a trial lawyer. I never thought anything like this would come from my stage career and motherhood. But I drew upon my ability to create a story each time I stood in front of a jury. With my ability to create suspense and foster empathy, I helped the jury members see my defendant's point of view. Another tactic I took from the stage and brought into the courtroom was my costume."

At the word 'costume,' Nicki used air quotes. She paused and rearranged the laptop and cell phone on her desk. The silence stretched between us. Was she trying to get back to work? Should I leave? I shuffled in my chair.

Nikki looked up and slid her devices away from her. "Sorry, just muting my phone, we don't need any interruptions. Now, where were we?"

"The . . . costume."

She smiled at me. "Ah, yes. My costume for the courthouse was conservative, but with flair. I always wore an eye-catcher: something for the judge and jury to keep their focus. On stage, I learned I needed to be the center of attention. When I was presenting in court, it was no different."

Nicki looked me in the eye. "Appearance and storytelling are critical if you want to advance your career. But they weren't the only reasons I advanced faster than some of my colleagues. I'll tell you about one of them, Stu. He had so much potential." Nicki stopped and shook her head in disappointment.

"Are you writing this down? It's important." Nicki looked at my notebook. "Stu was a great lawyer, but he focused on his past accomplishments. His degree was more important than his trials. He always complained about our employer, saying that the law firm he'd come from was much better. The situation got out of hand, and many of us started to avoid Stu. Rumor has it, the boss stopped him in the hallway and flat out told Stu, 'We don't care about your past. Identifying with your old job stops you from making progress. Put your attention on what you'll do for us in the future.' I was glad I never told my supervisors much of my past and especially thankful I used a stage name so they couldn't find me on social media."

Nicki flicked her short hair and said, "This is the third reason I excelled while others didn't: I showed I cared about our team. One Saturday night, five years into my career, I got a panicked phone call from a junior paralegal named Britley. I figured something must be wrong because we were friends at work, but we didn't hang out with one another on the weekends. She sobbed into the phone, telling me she dyed her hair at home, fallen asleep, and now her hair was green. I suggested she try to wash it, but she'd already tried that six times. It was still light green. She sent me a picture of the disastrous result. I told her to relax, come to work on Monday, and I would make everything alright. The next day, I contacted the lawyers, paralegals, and secretaries and asked them to come into work early. I protected their business clothes and used temporary green hair dye. Except on the main partner—he got a bright orange make-over." Britley came to our first meeting, wearing a fashionable hat. She looked at us with our business suits and weird hair and laughed. She felt a part of the team, and the incident brought everyone closer. It's essential to care for one another. Britley is still with us, and her hair is once again a natural color."

Nicki's action steps

- ✓ Use body language to match the mood and tone of your talk.
- ✓ Make yourself appear larger (more powerful) when you sit and walk.
- ✓ Use slow, controlled movements.
- ✓ As you talk, read the crowd and make adjustments.
- ✓ Don't hesitate when talking. Be heard.
- ✓ Use stories for parts you want people to remember.
- ✓ Let people draw conclusions from the stories—no need to tell them the point.
- ✓ Incorporate humor.
- ✓ During meetings, be present and engaged. Leave the cell phone in a different room.
- ✓ Add a bit of flair to your outfit—a splash of color or accent jewelry.
- ✓ Instead of focusing on your past accomplishments, focus on what you can do for the company.
- ✓ Keep negative or questionable images or comments out of social media.
- ✓ Show your team you care about them.

Three top take-aways from rocker, lawyer, and mother: Nicki

Be thoughtful of your body language and what it says about you as a professional.

Incorporate humorous stories people can picture to get your points across.

Be empathetic—show your team you care about them by giving your time, listening, and sharing your vulnerabilities.

Emma robbed Simon Sinek and it made her a great public speaker

I let out a sigh of relief as I entered Emma's cool, air-conditioned office. Even for California, it was a sweltering day. Emma brushed her blonde hair out of her face, smiled, and joined me at her floor-to-ceiling window looking out over San Francisco Bay.

"Amazing, isn't it?" she said in her soft English accent. "I moved here when I was only seventeen, but I still can't believe I get to live in this fantastic location. Please, take a seat." Her brown eyes sparkled, and I couldn't help smiling back. We walked over to her desk and took our seats. As I pulled out my leather-bound notebook, she began talking.

"I usually don't meet for these types of things. But your letter seemed genuine, and you flattered me by asking for my advice on public speaking. Talking on YouTube videos and at board-of-director meetings didn't come easily. I had to learn the tricks, the life-hacks, and the secrets." She paused and squinted at me.

"I have a secret that has helped me immensely. I don't usually speak about it, but you don't work in this city, so I suppose it can't hurt. I stole something and use it every time I present."

I raised my eyebrows, wanting to hear about Emma's theft.

"But before we get to that, I'll start with the most important aspects of public speaking. Come up with a short, clear headline. Repeat this tag-line within your presentation. When people leave, they have one concise message they can repeat and share." Emma stood and walked over to the window.

She faced away from me, but I could still hear her. "Tell the audience how your product solves the problem. Repeat that message with passion in two different ways. State why it's a problem. Then present a solution with short, concise sentences making things easy to understand." She stopped and turned toward me, pausing.

"Do you ever notice the great speakers always use the rule of three? They have three themes, three levels, three main points. People gravitate toward this rule. If you have more than three things you need to get across, cluster them to make three main parts." Emma smiled at me again.

"You got that?" She asked. "Short headline, you can repeat, powerful message about how your product solves the audience's problems, and the rule of three."

I nodded, scribbling in my notebook as fast as I could.

"Okay then, time to let you in on my secret. I had a professional crush on Simon Sinek. He's a great speaker. Simon is who I modeled when I practiced my talks. Anyone can find someone to emulate. Notice, I said emulate, not imitate. Imitate is second-rate. Develop and showcase your quirks and uniqueness. To make yourself comfortable, copy their exact movements. Practice those movements. Visualize yourself and go out and do it. An actor or athlete puts on a mask before showtime— they act the part. Most people aren't comfortable giving a presentation. They practice, and then they put on a face that isn't their own, and they perform. I'll tell you this much. All successful speakers have rituals: athletes, speakers, corporate executives, everyone who performs regularly in front of crowds. For example, Anthony Robbins bounces on a small trampoline to pump himself up. Or a golfer's ritual: two practice swings, then hit." Emma paused.

She shook her head and continued, "Speaking of golf, I'll go ahead and tell you the story of why I stole something from Simon Sinek. My dad was pretty good at golf. One year, he had the chance to buy some used clubs from a famous golfer. The pro was about the same height, so Dad didn't even have to make adjustments. He spent a bunch of money on them, so he called it his birthday gift to himself. The clubs weren't better quality than his regular set, but he played much better with them, just because a famous golfer had used them. My dad called it 'positive contagion.' It was the same for me: I needed something to remind me to be the best public speaker, but unlike my dad, I stole it. Early on in my career, I went to see Simon Sinek talk. It was a full conference, and his speech was fantastic. He used all the tricks I mentioned, plus a powerful stance, with equal weight on both legs. Did you know that when he feels uncomfortable, he rubs his right leg?" Emma looked up, her eyes glazed. "Ah, I will remember that talk forever. Simon made me fall in love with public speaking." She paused. "After the talk, he sat down at my table to watch the other speakers. He was taking notes in a book like yours."

Emma pointed toward my notebook. "In a break between speakers, Simon and I started talking about some of the key points. As he looked away towards the stage, I switched pens with him. Oh, I was smooth. I stole Simon Sinek's pen, and he didn't even realize it." Emma walked to her desk and came back with an ordinary ball-point pen. "This is the pen. Ever since that day, I have had this pen in my pocket for every presentation, YouTube video, and news conference. I'm not stupid. I know it doesn't have some special power, but it reminds me to present like Simon. Like my dad using the golf clubs in the same way the professional would have done."

Emma walked back to her desk and put the pen away. She smoothed her skirt and sat back down. "Over the years, I've perfected my presentation skills to match those of my role model. One big piece of the puzzle is using your body language to match the message you're trying to get across. Choose a style for your message. The colors used in your presentation and your outfit must match the tone. You wouldn't wear a clown outfit at a funeral." Emma stopped speaking and looked toward me.

She pointed to my notebook. "It's great that you're writing everything down. Your notebook is the best tool. The executives who move up carry a nice notebook. Like you, they take notes in it—jot down ideas. During meetings, they write down the important parts they hear and questions that come up. This way, they can reword the questions before they ask. Their notebook and their posture proves to the speaker they're listening. When you're listening in a meeting, sit upright and keep alert. Posture will improve how you're perceived. It will show you're engaged and willing to take risks. And that is what upper management wants—people who take risks to make the company more money. The best assignments go to those who show engagement with their posture and take hand-written notes. I can't answer why. It's one of those little-known life-hacks."

I looked up at Emma with a frown. "I missed the previous bit, could you repeat it?"

"Of course. Let's use the rule of three one more time. Here are your three main points to remember from the second half of this discussion," she said. "Use a positive contagion, match your body language to your message, and stay alert by taking notes and keeping great posture."

"Thanks. That's very clear," I said, writing the key points down. "This has been great, Emma. I can't thank you enough."

Emma's action steps

- ✓ When presenting, repeat your short headline so people will remember it.
- ✓ With passion, tell the audience why there is a problem and how your product solves it.
- ✓ Use the rule of 3 themes—if more, cluster.
- ✓ Keep it simple, be concise: shorter words, shorter sentences.
- ✓ Find and use a positive contagion: owning something from an idol.
- ✓ Use rituals and beliefs to overcome the fear of failure, like an athlete performing a routine.
- ✓ Model people who do it well—watch their exact movements, practice the moves, visualize you doing the actions, then do them yourself.
- ✓ Put on the mask, then act the part.
- ✓ Choose the style best suited for the presentation; match the tone with colors and body language.
- ✓ Stand with equal weight on both feet.
- ✓ Use a notebook of essential take-aways and write down questions before asking.
- ✓ Use good posture and hand-written notes to show you are engaged.
- ✓ Appear engaged
- ✓ Be willing to take calculated risks.
- ✓ Take hand-written notes.

Three top take-aways from Emma

Find and emulate a public speaker you feel is effective at reaching the audience.

Bring a notebook to meetings and take hand-written notes. Leave your phone and computer in your office.

Keep good posture. Add a reminder, like a bracelet, to focus on sitting up straight and walking tall.

Marc wouldn't give Devon a positive recommendation

"Every time I tried to leap, I got slammed down on the ground, like a sacked quarterback." Devon threw up his hands and grimaced, his brown eyes squinting at me. "I had made it pretty high in the organization, but I was ready for more. I wanted a big office with the side door to escape. My first boss had one of them, and ever since, it's stuck with me as a marker of success. I always found it so cool: if someone came to my secretary and wouldn't leave, I could just escape."

Devon tilted his head upwards and scratched at the stubble on his cheek.

"One time, I was trying for the senior position at another branch of our office," he continued. "I thought the interview went well. Then I got the letter I was so familiar with. 'We are going in a different direction.' I called the person who interviewed me and asked to meet for lunch at an Italian place called Antonio's. We ordered some pizza, and I went for it straight away. 'What do I need to do to get to the next level?' I asked."

Devon paused and took a drink of his iced Coke. "At the restaurant, the interviewer asked me what my personal vision statement was? What was I trying to achieve professionally? To be completely honest, my goal was to get respect as the leader of the organization. But I wasn't about to tell that to the interviewer, and I didn't have anything intelligent I could share. As I sat there dumbfounded, the interviewer continued, 'If you're not sure, your employers won't be, either,'" Devon shook his head in quiet disbelief.

I interjected in agreement, "He had a good point: If you don't have a clear purpose, there's no reason to earn a promotion. People use personal vision statements to stay focused on completing essential tasks. For example, Oprah Winfrey's vision is: To be a teacher. And to be known for inspiring her students to be more than they thought they could be (Winfrey, 2020). Such a vision statement can be an ingenious way of introducing yourself.'"

The phone rang, and Devon picked it up. I looked around the airy room and made a note into my leather-bound book. When I looked up again, Devon was standing in front of me, hand outstretched. "Hi, I'm Devon. My mission is to create work environments that foster satisfaction, creativity, and growth." He looked me in the eyes, shook my hand, then sat back down.

"You see how this speaks volumes of who I am and what's important to me. It's a quirky way to introduce myself and make sure people don't forget me. This phrase aligns my head, mouth, heart, and actions." He paused.

"Before I paid the bill at Antonio's, I asked the interviewer one last question. 'What else should I do to figure out why I can't move up?' He told me to find out how I'm perceived. I needed to ask my boss for specific feedback and find out which metrics are most important by asking to see my performance review. Once I knew them, I should ask veteran employees what's important to focus on at the company, then over perform in those areas to add value to the organization. We left the restaurant, and I set a meeting with Marc, my supervisor."

Devon stood up and paced up and down the room. "I should have met with Marc two years earlier. As it turns out, he thought of me as an ungrateful spotlight hog." Devon paused and shook his head as if he was mad at himself.

He picked up an autographed football from a case and threw it from one hand to the other. "Each year, I went to an annual review with Marc. I brought in my folder of the year's accomplishments. To me, it was quantifiable proof I was performing higher than expected, but Marc got the impression I was trying to take all the credit for projects. He was right. I downplayed the team aspect and tried to make myself look like the breadwinner. I should've spoken well about my teammates."

Devon walked back over to the case and put down the football. He turned and said, "Marc started with some positive things. He liked how I moved team discussions forward. He appreciated how I asked a take-away question at the onset of meetings. Then he tore me down, telling me I was ungrateful. He had gotten me my last promotion, and I didn't utter a word of thanks. I thought I earned that promotion, and it wasn't a gift from Marc, but I could've still shown my appreciation. To tell you the truth, I had trouble with gratitude. Teammates would go to bat for me, and I expected it as part of work. I needed to be more empathetic."

Devon returned to his desk. "Once you speak, you can't take it back. But you could've delayed saying it. One time my boss came to me and asked me to do this mundane task. I told him, 'That's not my job.' That was a mistake. I would've been better off keeping my mouth shut and finding out why he asked me to do it. Another time, the entire team was working late on a Friday night. In my frustration, I said, 'My lousy salary isn't enough for this!' Many of my junior teammates earned half as much as I did, so it was an insensitive thing to say."

Devon shrugged and looked at me. "Sometimes, it's best to keep your comments to yourself. You see this on TV—a detective usually waits to give an official message to the press. But not me, I would snap to a decision and bite heads off. I assumed the worst and accused people of screwing up when I should have asked questions and delayed my response until I had time to consider all aspects. I should have asked for the other person's perspective."

Devon paused again, gazing out of the window. I had already started to put away my notebook when he spoke up again, "After finding out how Marc perceived me, I needed to get out. I would never get a promotion with him leading the charges against me. There was too much bad history to overcome. I put in for a lateral transfer and changed who I was. I developed my emotional intelligence and finally got the promotion I longed for."

As I finished my notes, Devon stood up and sauntered towards the bookcase. "Lovely to meet you," he said with a smile. "But it's time for me to head off." He waved, then pushed his hand against the case. A hidden door swung open, and he walked out, shutting it firmly behind him.

Devon's action steps

- ✓ Use appropriate body language when you're making a point.
- ✓ Be direct—ask for what you need.
- ✓ Move discussions forward.
- ✓ Use take-away questions at the beginning of your presentations.
- ✓ Create a personal vision statement.
- ✓ Focus your work around your vision statement to align your head, mouth, heart, and actions.
- ✓ Use your vision statement to introduce yourself.
- ✓ At reviews, bring quantified evidence of your accomplishments.
- ✓ Be humble and share your accomplishments as a team effort.
- ✓ Give specific credit to the team for the work, using names and how they contributed.
- ✓ Ask for specific and honest feedback from supervisors and friends.
- ✓ Find out how you're perceived by asking colleagues and superiors.
- ✓ Be thankful, show your appreciation for coworkers.
- ✓ Express empathy when work friends have a hard time.
- ✓ Don't say something until you have all the facts—you can't take back something said, but you could've delayed announcing it.
- ✓ Learn to express your emotional intelligence.
- ✓ If you can't overcome how you were once perceived, cut ties, reinvent yourself, and start new somewhere else.

Devon's top three

Ask for what you need.

Create a personal vision statement that can guide your professional life.

Develop your emotional intelligence—those who have the highest emotional intelligence advance the quickest.

II
Get the job done

Those people who can get the job done on-time and error-free, earn the promotions.

Michelle helped young people find their purpose

"How do we keep the young generation happy at work? It's not all about egg-shaped chairs and Kombucha." Michelle said as we sauntered along her firm's hallway towards her office. Her watch glistened as she gestured for me to enter the spacious room. Seeing my curious glance, she smiled and said: "It's a Cartier Crash."

Michelle was a vice-president in an industry that relied on young, energetic new hires. With her flawless caramel skin and immaculate make-up and hair, she appeared more youthful than her forty-five years.

I sat down in one of the minimalist grey armchairs, but she remained standing in front of a conference table. "We hire workers out of college and even high school. Years ago, we would look for the right candidate with the knowledge, skill, and training to get the job done. We didn't want to spend time and money trying to train people. We wanted results from the hire. We wanted to see a return on our investment immediately."

Michelle straightened her dress and gestured towards a door on the opposite end of the room. I stood back up and walked towards it. "These trained hires didn't want to work. They only wanted money and often quit after a few months. I had human resources do exit interviews with them. Some left for typical reasons, a major change in life, such as getting married. But most indicated people didn't like them at work, or they felt their job lacked purpose."

After we walked through the conference room door, we came to a large window overlooking cubicles with workers. We could just make out the heated telephone discussions, the tapping of dozens of keyboards, and the whirring of the printer, but the glass softened the sounds. "To try to remedy the problem, we stopped hiring and spent two years employing freelance workers. They, too, wouldn't last for more than a handful of months." We strode on in silence for what seemed like the length of a football field.

We came to a bridge overlooking the front entrance and the security guards sitting beneath us. "Eventually, we went back to hiring, but this time it was different. We didn't care about their skill, training, or previous experience with a similar product. Instead, we focused our search on personality types. Do you know how some people have a diligent work attitude? No matter what, they will do their best work at the position they're in—work harder, longer. These same people will view a less desirable position as a growth opportunity where they learn and develop their skills. These were the people we were after—the ones we wanted to groom for the position."

Michelle pointed to the front entrance as a young man walked in. He shifted uncomfortably in his suit and looked around nervously until the security guard called him over. "We put new hires through our university. Eight weeks to train for the job."

She crossed the bridge, and we reached another conference room, large enough for 20 people. On the walls were signs and posters.

'What's your superpower?'

'How do your virtues relate to the company's mission?'

'Mistakes happen; it's your way of growing.'

'It's 11:00, do you know where your phone is?'

As I scanned the room, I realized we weren't alone. In the corner stood a woman, half-hidden behind a curtain. I moved closer to see who was in there. I must have had a quizzical look on my face as I saw someone with Michelle's hair and an outfit like she would wear. But the woman didn't move.

"I noticed you found the mannequin in the corner."

I jumped and turned around to stare at Michelle, who chuckled.

"I thought . . ." I stammered.

"I have an evil twin?" She grinned. "We use the mannequin as a visual tool in our university. It reminds people how we want them to dress. Notice I don't have a cell phone in my hand—that's a reminder too. We don't want distractions that prevent people from being social. Even when phones are on silent, people stay on alert to cater to potential messages."

Michelle swung her wrist up and shook her watch. "See my Cartier Crash? We encourage our new hires to find something they can wear. A reminder to focus on their personal mission statement, their superpower, and virtues." Michelle let her fingers glide over the watch's curved surface. "I have mine. When I have a difficult decision, I look at my left wrist. Seeing my watch helps remind me to focus on my mission statement, virtues, and superpower as I make that decision. Each time people come into this conference room, they get a reminder of the tool we used to train them, me."

Michelle nodded her chin in the direction of the posters. "Our university develops great employees and helps people become happier with their life. We help them grow as humans by showing them their own strengths and virtues. To achieve this, our instructors give them strength finders and help them to create their own personal vision statement. Everyone has a superpower. It's just a matter of finding it through their strengths and virtues. Then we connect their purpose and personal vision to the mission of the firm."

She looked up at me. "We want confident workers. Those who focus on what they do best are the most confident. Using their strengths to showcase confidence can propel entry-level employees to an executive position within a few short years. We have a team to help our recruits narrow down their vision statement so they can use it to introduce themselves." Michelle stood opposite me and looked me in the eyes. She held out her hand to shake mine. "Hi, my name is Michelle. I help people realize that getting negative feedback is a faster way to grow."

She smiled, then dropped her hand back down. "We want our employees to know their work is meaningful. They need to see the positive impact they have outside of the company. Once a month, we have a company-wide meeting to share stories about how our employees helped the customers. The response is fantastic, and everyone works hard all month to be able to share a great story. Sometimes, we even bring in customers to share the impact our products have had in their lives."

We turned the corner and started to walk toward her office.

At the door, Michelle paused and turned to face me again. She put her hand on the door handle but didn't open it. "No one can have their cell phone in a meeting—it stays in their office. Same thing if you're eating lunch with a coworker. Remember how people quit because they didn't feel supported by their peers? That's because they didn't build relationships. No one talked with one another. They spent all their time on their cell phone—before a meeting, during a meeting, and at lunch. Some have taken this no cell phone policy to heart even in their private life. They leave it in the car while they're out on a date or at dinner with friends. I've heard they even got their friends to do the same. How can you quit a job where your best friend still works? We insist they strike a balance between cell phone and in-person dialogue."

Michelle opened her office door, and we walked inside toward two comfortable chairs. She handed me a bottle of water. "Another thing we try to avoid is scaring people into working. We want to make everyone feel safe. Cooperation is more important than results. That's not to say we don't expect excellence—it's not an act but a habit. And if you get in the habit of delivering better than expected results, we'll have the type of employees we need."

Michelle's action steps

- ✓ Work diligently.
- ✓ Do your best work, no matter your position.
- ✓ View a lower position as an opportunity to grow, learn, and develop skills.
- ✓ Work harder, longer, smarter than your peers.
- ✓ Excellence is not an act, but a habit—get in the habit of delivering better than expected results.
- ✓ Wear something to remind you of your mission/vision statement.
- ✓ Focus on what you do best and showcase it to demonstrate confidence and skill.
- ✓ Use negative feedback to develop and grow.
- ✓ Build relationships by leaving your cell phone behind during person to person meetings.

Three top take-aways from Michelle

Focus and capitalize on your strengths. Outsource time-consuming tasks you aren't good at or don't enjoy.

View feedback as a learning opportunity. Realize negative feedback is the company's way to get you to grow.

Build positive relationships at work.

Rob carjacked an old lady

"This is beautiful, it feels like the countryside," I said. Rob smiled down at me as we walked along the nature trail in the heart of Los Angeles. At six foot five, he towered over me. We strolled in silence for several minutes, listening to the birds chirping and the distant rumble of traffic.

Finally, he spoke up. "Disorganization was my greatest fault. Was I smart? Yes. But was I someone who could visualize the future and plan for it? Definitely not."

He sighed. "I'll give you an example of how scatter-brained I was. Back then, I was living in a small city. Usually, I would get a cup of coffee from a place a block away from my apartment, then catch public transportation to work. On busy days, I grabbed an Uber or Lyft. This particular morning, the line at the coffee shop was long. By the time I got near the counter, I knew I would miss my regular bus, so I ordered an Uber. My phone indicated I would see a silver Honda Civic in nine minutes—perfect timing. I got my coffee and walked outside and, sure enough, a silver Honda Civic pulled up. I jumped in the back, surprised that the driver was an old, nervous-looking lady. She asked where to—like she didn't know. I told her, and she kept asking for driving directions. I assumed her cell phone wasn't working, so I told her how to get to the office. When we got there, I got out and thanked her. As I pulled out my phone to leave a tip and a decent review, I realized my driver marked me as a 'no-show' and canceled my ride. I had car-jacked a little old lady in a Honda Civic."

"Wow, that's crazy. But now, you're one of the most organized people I've met! Your schedule is packed, but you were still able to fit me in," I said. "What changed?"

"I started planning the end, setting goals for everything. Things won't go as planned, but you can always adjust to meet the circumstances. I always set my goals first. Then I calendarize them. Let me explain the difference between using a calendar and a to-do list." Rob paused and pulled out his cell phone and tapped it. "Calendars are better at making sure you have enough time to complete the task. To-do lists don't work because people focus on checking off tasks and start with the easiest ones. Then, they are already tired by the time they attempt the hard tasks, so they push them to another day. Executives use a calendar, so they know they have time to complete the tasks."

As we walked on, Rob slid the phone from one hand to the other, then unlocked it and held it up. "Put your long-term and short-term goals on your calendar." He opened his virtual calendar, marked in five different colors. "I wasn't always this organized. Five years ago, I thought I had it all figured out and deserved a promotion. When I failed, I took a step back. I knew I wanted to move up the corporate ladder, but I just didn't know how to get there. I started to research how those people in power make everything happen, and I took every piece of their advice. I put a meeting on my calendar to ask for a promotion—two years out. I then started to build up the skills I would need for that position. I calendarized getting those skills too. I took classes. My communication style, my abilities, I improved it all." He paused and slid his phone back into his pocket. "It worked."

We passed a little lake, and Rob gazed out at it, then turned to face me. "Sales and management are where companies spend money. These are the two spots to get the highest salaries. It's where companies make their profit. A year after I started building up my skills for the promotion, I communicated my ambition to everyone I met at the company. It might seem counterintuitive, but I started to say 'no.' I chose not to get involved with specific projects. I focused all my actions on what I wanted to become. I cut out, said 'no,' to the rest."

Rob stood and took off his sports jacket. "What's your best time of day? When do you complete your best work?"

He pointed at me but didn't pause to let me answer. "Only make difficult decisions during this time of day. Reserve it to get your best work done. Don't let distractions seep in and ruin your prime-time. Instead, use it to answer those tough emails, decide who gets promoted and which projects get tabled. If a decision comes up and it's not during your best time, postpone your response until the next day. You don't have to tell everyone your secret. Postponing your response will make you look strategic and wise."

Rob got his phone out again and turned it towards me as we started to climb a hill. "See these evaluations? I get great marks from the boss, but they mean nothing to me. I set my own goals and my own scorecard because true motivation comes from within. People praising or criticizing you could have a double motive, so ignore the cheers and the 'boo's.' People who criticize me don't realize my decisions come from my dignity, values, and virtues. If I keep those three things in mind for every decision, I won't care what the critics say." He paused at the top of the hill and waited for me to catch up.

"Do you work out?" he continued. I nodded and shrugged my shoulders, still too out of breath to speak.

"I don't work out very often, but when I do, I go with a buddy. He's strong. Stronger than me. If I evaluated myself based on his ability, I would fail every time, but I keep my scorecard, and he keeps his. I push myself based on my abilities and strengths."

We strolled down the hill, and I realized that we were back at the start of the trail. We'd completed the loop, and our hour was up. "I have to go to a meeting now. It was good to talk with you," Rob said. "But I have one last piece of advice you need. Set a goal, so you know when to stop. You need to recognize when enough is enough. I had an ambitious friend. He never set his end-goal. Nothing was enough for him. He kept at it until he lost it all: family, his wealth, his reputation. Know when enough is enough and stop."

With that, he waved, turned, and walked back towards the hustle and bustle of the city center.

Rob's action steps

- ✓ Calendarize your long and short goals.
- ✓ Set a plan to build the skills to move up in 2-3 years.
- ✓ Communicate your ambitions.
- ✓ Refuse those projects that don't correspond to what you want to become.
- ✓ Make difficult decisions, and do your best work during your prime-time.
- ✓ Postpone your response to come across as strategic and wise.
- ✓ Use a personal scorecard: ignore the cheers and criticism.
- ✓ Set a goal so you can stop and know when enough is enough.

Rob's favorite three take-aways

Use a calendar, not a to-do-list.

Be picky about which projects to take. Look for the projects that will give you a visible win.

Come across as strategic and wise by postponing your responses to difficult questions until you can think about it during your best time of day.

Heather lost her job because she solved problems

"You'd think a problem solver would be an asset to a company. Not at my company—they fired me." Heather brushed back her curly hair and picked up her cup of coffee. "The problem was the way I went about solving problems."

She gazed at me as I pulled out my leather-bound notebook. "Volunteering for high-visibility, high-priority projects shot me up the corporate ladder. I took the initiative. I did things not asked of me, and I got the job done." Heather lifted her chin and straightened her back. She slid her chair away from her glass top table, her spine perfectly erect.

"I messed up in a few ways. Because of those problems, I lost my job." Her expression fell. "I'm fine now. I got another job. I'm better off because I learned my lesson. In my previous job, I didn't align my priorities with what was important for my boss. If I had realized the direction she wanted to move the company, I would've changed. Instead, I pushed projects that weren't important to the big picture." Heather stood and walked over to a glass bookshelf. She wiped at a speck of dust, then turned back towards me.

"One thing I learned early on is the importance of preparing for failure. Before each presentation or roll-out of a new product, you have to have contingency plans. Think about what objections people might have. Every situation needs a back-up plan. I call it premortem—pretend it failed. Patch the holes before the roll-out, presentation, or objections come your way. This focus on the premortem has always been my great strength. Because this provided so much value to the company, my boss initially ignored my two big flaws: using negative language and not focusing on what's important to the firm."

Heather moved from her bookcase over to the window. I looked out past her at the tall building right across the street, where a row of office workers sat at their computers.

"Nice view," I said, as one of the men from the next building stared at me with a vacant gaze.

Heather smiled. "It's got its perks. The buildings are too close, but at least I'm never lonely." She paused. "I often chose my words poorly. My mistake was saying, 'It will fail because . . . ' When what I should have said was 'to play devil's advocate.' This phrasing would've let people know I believe in their hard work and am only trying to make it better. I was the negative one, not the problem solver. My negativity and not having the same vision as my boss got me fired at the worst possible time, the year I bought a house and got married."

Heather sat back down and slumped for the first time. "It was the Friday before Thanksgiving week. We were in a meeting planning holiday parties. Last year a guy named Brian got drunk and made a fool of himself. He made everyone at the party feel uncomfortable. I said, 'We don't want Brian vomiting on everyone's shoes again. We better limit how much people drink.' The boss asked to talk with me outside the conference room. I never returned." Heather looked up at me.

"That seems harsh," I said.

She shook her head. "It was only the drop that made the bucket overflow. I had it coming. Luckily, I had a premortem plan for termination too. Step one was to figure out what I did wrong—patch the hole. Fix me. The biggest gift from that layoff was learning humility. I should have been honest about my flaws and what I needed to work on so people could relate to me better. In this new role, I'm open about my mistakes, fears, and uncertainties, making me more trustworthy. I've also learned a better way of communicating my premortem concerns."

Heather went to her desk and rummaged around for a bit. She pulled out an ivory-colored paper. She handed it to me. On one side was hand-written notes. "When they fired me, I started to write out important aspects to who I was and how I acted. At first, it was long. My goal was to get it to one page. You can keep it. Maybe use it for your book."

When I looked up from her notes, Heather was smirking.

"What's up?" I asked.

"I just remembered something that happened three months after I started working here," she said. "People had started to get to know me, and I already had the reputation of the woman who looked at things from every angle. It was the week before the launch of this big project. Our team of 12 people had worked on for months. We were in a meeting waiting for the boss. I had bought 25 pieces of edible paper. I gave two pieces to each team member. As the boss walked in, we were all eating the paper with stacks of other papers below it. Someone shouted around a mouth full of paper, 'Heather found a fatal flaw in the plan. We're scrapping the whole thing.' I nodded eagerly and added, 'The whole thing won't work, we have to destroy it.' The boss started to laugh, and I began to fit in."

Heather's action steps

- ✓ Volunteer for high-visibility, high-priority projects.
- ✓ Take the initiative—do things not asked of you.
- ✓ Get the job done.
- ✓ Align your priorities with the priorities of your supervisor.
- ✓ Prepare for failure and create contingency plans.
- ✓ Speak up. Be candid in a helpful way.
- ✓ Don't be negative all the time.
- ✓ Be humble in front of coworkers.
- ✓ Be honest about your flaws.
- ✓ Give credit where it's due.
- ✓ Be open about your mistakes, fears, and uncertainties.
- ✓ Have light-hearted fun in the office. Show people your sense of humor.

Heather's advice

The premortem: For your next presentation or project, visualize failure. Write down in detail:
- ಇ What happened? How exactly did you fail?
- ಇ Why? What was the issue?
- ಇ What did you do to fix it?
- ಇ Finally, summarize in 2-4 sentences what you will do differently to plan for and guard yourself against this type of failure.

Speak to your boss. Set up a meeting to discuss your current or future project. Ask:
- What is the aim of this project, and how will it benefit the firm?
- What aspect of the project do I need to focus on to make it a success?
- What is the best possible outcome you could imagine, and how can I make this happen?

Write down three recent moments when you experienced tension with your coworkers. Note down:
- What negative language did you use?
- How could you have changed your language to make it more positive?
- How could you have diffused the situation with humor?
- In the future, whenever such a situation comes up, repeat these steps. You will soon notice yourself reacting more positively at the moment.

Chad's unanswered emails solve their own problems

I power-walked down the street towards the little New Hampshire coffee shop, shivering in the brisk October air. Was I late? I glanced at my watch – 12:55 PM – and sped up even more. With two minutes to spare, I entered and immediately spotted a wiry middle-aged man waving at me.

"Hello, you must be Chad," I said as I approached his table.

He smiled and gestured at the chair next to him. "Please, take a seat. My wife Anne is just getting our drinks," he said.

I looked over to the line, where an athletic-looking woman with long brown hair stood. She was engrossed in her phone, tapping rapidly as the line shuffled forwards. Suddenly, she looked up and smiled at me, then turned her gaze back on her phone.

"She's just getting the last bit of work done," Chad explained. "After this, we're done for the day. Time for a bike ride, I think."

"Wow, you're done for the day already?" I raised my eyebrows. "It's a bit cold for a bike ride, though."

"Oh, we're used to this weather. Got some great gear." He patted his high-tech cycling jacket.

Anne returned with the coffees and pastries and sat down. The couple were both in their late forties and had separate, successful careers. They'd agreed to meet with me to discuss productivity tips for the workplace.

"My advice is unconventional," Chad started after Anne settled in her seat. "You won't hear many other people talk about this, but it's been the foundation of our lives for 15 years and allows us to enjoy more time together." He paused. "Force yourself to get done with your regular job in 80% of the time. Spend the extra hours on your goals, once you've reached them, spend more time with your loved ones." Chad sat back and took a sip of his mocha latte.

I nodded and took rapid notes in my black, leather-bound journal. Anne spoke up, "People fill up their time to make themselves feel busy and look useful. The difference between them and us: they want to appear busy, and we want to enjoy life."

She took a breath. "Three things help us to be more productive than everyone else: reduce useless activities, reduce interruptions, and work with time restrictions. Anyone can complete their job in 80% of the time if they follow these rules. Social media takes up time, and people do it during working hours as a stress reducer. But not getting done with work is why they're under stress. We cut out social media. Our true friends know how to reach us, and it's not through online posts or instant messages." Anne paused and got up to fetch some napkins while I finished taking notes.

When I looked up, Chad put his cup down and took a bite of a chocolate-filled croissant. After he chewed, he said, "Emails were my biggest distraction. The problem first caught my attention when I spent a week working from home. My desk was at the front of the house, overlooking the street, and I saw my neighbor when he came out to check his mailbox. 'This is odd,' I thought. 'The mailman hasn't even been here yet.' Ten minutes later, he came out again. Then, half an hour later. I saw him at least twenty times that day, checking his empty mailbox until the mailman finally came at lunchtime. 'He must be expecting a big check,' I thought. But Tuesday brought the same scene. On Wednesday, I used a stopwatch—he checked every 12 minutes for three hours. I talked to my wife about it that night, and she told me she'd noticed some other crazy behavior in our neighbor. On Thursday, he was out again, promptly at 9:00 AM, checking the mailbox. When I saw him that morning, it struck me that I had already checked my email twice. At 9:15, he was out again, and I had reviewed and responded to two emails between 9:00 and 9:15. Before 9:30, he was out there again. It dawned on me—I was checking email more often than he was checking the mailbox. Was I as crazy as my neighbor? On that Thursday, I checked my email 74 times. My neighbor checked his mailbox 17 times." Chad paused and took a sip of his coffee.

"The next Monday, I was back in the office, but I made the change. I now check email twice a day. I put a system into place to safeguard myself from missing an important message from a high-level executive. If I get an email from a senior executive, my cell phone notifies me. Those are rare, but I do give them the priority."

"That sounds like a great idea," I said.

"It works well for me." Chad tilted his head to the side. "I set up an auto-response which informs people I will answer their email within 12 hours and how to get ahold of me in case of an emergency. Do you know what happens when someone sends me a problem via email, and I don't get back to them right away?" I shrugged my shoulder.

"80% of the problems get solved without me. By delaying my response, difficulties get resolved." Chad paused very briefly, leaning towards me.

"My prime-time is in the mornings. I have a routine. I get up before anyone else and set myself a 90-minute timer to get done with the work that needs my full attention. Early morning is my uninterrupted time, and I don't allow any distractions. Whenever your prime-time is, safe-guard it to get your best work done. Did you know, people can only have an intense focus for five hours a day? Why not spend your best five hours working your job and then the rest of the time for yourself?"

Anne nodded. "Since implementing this, we have a great work-life balance," she observed.

"Before I started getting done with my job by noon concept, I worked all day," Chad said. "At night, I would come home exhausted. Too worn out to even be nice to my wife." Chad looked over at Anne, who gave a slight shrug.

Chad continued, "One night, I agreed to make dinner. I needed something easy because I was beat-tired as usual. I pulled out chicken nuggets from the freezer." Anne giggled, anticipating the rest of Chad's story. "I set the timer for the oven and put in the nuggets. Then I put some salad dressings in small bowls, microwaved green beans, and added garlic salt. The timer went off, and I gasped at the mess in the oven. The chicken nuggets had melted all over the oven dish. That's when I realized I'd accidentally put cookies into the oven instead of nuggets."

Chad shook his head, and Anne chuckled. "That night, we ate green beans and cookies for dinner," she said.

Chad gave a bit of a snort and resumed his story, "The cookie incident was one of the deciding factors in my decision to change my life. That's when I implemented my 90-minute rule. After checking my emails in the morning, I spend time on the ones that don't resolve themselves, which usually require a great deal of thought. I need to be at my best when making these decisions. That's why I use mornings. By lunchtime, I've completed all my work, and the rest of the day is mine. I start every day at 5:00 AM and only take one break for breakfast and commuting to work. That way, I can start wrapping things up as people are leaving for lunch. Before I take off, I have my second round of answering emails." Chad picked up the remains of his croissant and popped it in his mouth.

"Chad also eliminated the junk emails by unsubscribing and using folders," Anne said. "He has a Friday folder for emails that can wait until the end of the week. He sends a quick reply, something like: 'I agree, we need to address this, but I'm working on other tasks and want to give it some thought. I'll get back to you by Friday afternoon.' On Friday, he gets around to them." Anne paused and looked at Chad, who nodded.

"I personally never had a problem with emails taking up my time," she continued. "But I knew I wasn't as efficient as I could be, so I decided to measure where my time was going. For one week, I used a stopwatch on my phone to track the time I was wasting. It turns out, colleagues at work were the number one problem. I'm all about being nice, but there is a limit. I don't want to be interrupted to listen to a story about someone's husband licking their baby."

My head snapped up, and I took in Chad's wrinkled forehead.

"Uh, what?" he said.

"Okay, I'll tell you the story. This coworker, the most talkative person I know, had a baby almost a year ago. One day, she came into my office and started to tell me about her weekend adventure. She was in the kitchen cleaning up, and her husband was in the family room, eating a hotdog and holding the baby. He was watching football when a glob of mustard spilled out of the hotdog bun onto the baby's forehead. When the mother walked in, she saw her husband licking the baby clean." She paused and frowned at Chad and me as we tried to stifle our snorts. "I mean, who has time to listen to that?"

Anne leaned forward. "Anyway, the stopwatch experiment taught me to set aside some dedicated time for conversations instead of allowing people to distract me all day. I take a twenty-minute break every day to spend with my colleagues, but when I'm working, I don't allow interruptions anymore. Another huge waste of time was my car commute. I realized I had other ways to get to work, like the train. It wasn't as convenient to use public transportation, but it allowed me to use that time. I had plenty of time for mundane tasks during my commute." Anne pointed to the line of people waiting for coffees. "As I wait for the train or in line, I answer my emails. Now, I don't mind waiting. I always get things done."

Chad cleared his throat. "Cut losing projects," he said. "People feel they have to continue with their plans because they've already sunk so much time into it. If you know the outcome is going to be bad, cut it as soon as possible. Have you ever been bowling?"

"I love bowling," I replied and smiled.

"You know how the ball returns have these rounded hoods? Well, my first managerial job was for this company that made parts for bowling alleys. I was overseeing the production of these ball return covers. When I first started, upper management was upset. We had so many at the end of the line with defects. These hoods would go through a six-step process. At three of those stages, things could get seriously messed up—to the point the hoods didn't fit our standards. To solve the problem, we implemented a stricter elimination process. I went to each line worker and told him, 'If you see a hood that doesn't reach our standard, pull it from the process—scrap it.' The guy pulling them from the forms found the most, and the employee in charge of sanding picked the ones he knew he wouldn't be able to trim enough to make them look right. By the time the hoods reached polishing, only the best had gotten through. After cutting the losers, the inspector could report we were making good use of our time." Chad drank some more of his coffee, and Anne slid to the end of her chair.

"Chad is right, cutting your losses can save a lot of time," she said. "I learned that from the CEO in my company. When I first started working here, I asked him for book recommendations. He gave me three, and I read them all. The books helped enormously, but the relationship I developed with my boss was even more crucial. He appreciated how motivated and determined I was. Surround yourself with mentors and sponsors like this to form a like-minded community and learn from each other. They increase competition and accountability. Like a bike-riding group, they motivate and encourage one another. Reading the same books is a clever way to show upper management how serious you are about moving up. It also gives common ground to talk about."

Chad and Anne's action steps

- ✓ Streamline the amount of time you spend working.
- ✓ Cut out the time-consuming tasks that don't make a significant impact.
- ✓ Use the empty time, such as waiting in line, to complete work.
- ✓ With your extra time, accomplish your goals.
- ✓ Use prime-time to accomplish your challenging and essential tasks.

- ✓ Cut projects that won't have a dramatic impact.
- ✓ Use mentors and sponsors and get their book recommendations.

The top three take-aways from the coffee shop

Step 1: Reduce your working time by 20%. Start with the following adjustments:
- ○ Use the empty time, such as commuting and waiting in line, to get mundane tasks done. If you take your car to work, experiment with using public transport. Can you get things done on your commute?
- ○ Choose two set times a day to check your emails. If you get many unimportant messages, delay your response until the end of the week to see how many issues can be resolved without you.
- ○ Unsubscribe from email lists that don't provide you with value.
- ○ Create a daily 90-minute time slot for distraction-free work to complete your most demanding tasks. Let your coworkers know that you don't want to be distracted during this time.

Once you have reclaimed 20% of your time, use it to work on your goals. You can start with Step 2.

Step 2: Ask for book recommendations from the three people in your company or industry you admire the most. Buy and read the books, then ask meaningful questions or start a discussion to demonstrate you took their advice.

Step 3: Evaluate your current projects. What are the likely outcomes? Are any of them expected to fail? If so, cut your losses early and move on to a project with a higher chance for success.

Office politics gave Denzel power, but he had to learn the hard way

Denzel landed on his face outside the office doors because of office politics. "Security escorted me out of the building. I had a box of my personal belongings, and security had a hand on my shoulder. It was all over a vacant building and toxic, back-stabbing managers." Denzel got up, frustrated, then continued, "I was working at the office. I was the finance guy for this place—I controlled the purse strings. We were growing but not as fast as people thought. The building next to ours went vacant and then up for sale. One group in our organization wanted to buy it and move their section into the renovated space."

Denzel pointed at me and said, "You already realize there are cool and uncool groups. Some sections of the organization have the favor of the big boss, and others don't. The connected group has the ear of the CEO and usually get their way—that group wanted the property. They had a meeting without me to discuss it with the boss. The CEO told them to check with me to find out if it would be a good investment."

Denzel was pointing at himself and shaking his head. "They checked with me, and I told them I'd look into it. A few weeks later, I came to the conclusion we not only couldn't afford it, but the move would also stifle our growth. I told the cool group this, but it was my mistake to tell them without the CEO in the meeting. Those back-stabbers went behind me. They told the boss I was arrogant. They convinced my supervisor I wouldn't listen to constructive feedback. I would become defensive at the slightest remarks. For their final knife in my back, they told him I would take credit for other people's work, and push the blame onto others when it should have been all on me. The boss called me in on a Friday and fired me."

Denzel was upset as he told the story. He continued anyway, "Office politics come from scarce resources mixed with a variety of people with diverse perspectives on how to use those resources. It's employees trying to get power, prestige, or more money. In my case, the cool group wanted money and prestige. I should have realized it was the group the boss favored before I announced my decision."

Denzel walked to the door, took off his blazer, and hung it on a hook. As he walked back toward me, he showed me a skinny bracelet on his left wrist. Then said, "Where I am now, I'm better at playing the game. I wore this bracelet to remind me, 'always take the moral high ground and develop cooperation every day.'"

Denzel sat back down. He then continued, "I still wanted rapid advancement no matter where I got my next job. I developed a strategy. I realized who you know determines the projects you get, and I wanted the toughest. Do you know why? I needed to shine in the eyes of stakeholders and the direct reports under them." Denzel swiveled his chair back and forth. He then continued, "The higher-ups are the ones who can propel your career, and I needed them to see me at my best. I first analyzed the skills and personality they wanted in the next level up. I worked on developing those skills. I also communicated I had the skills through those tough projects. After each project, I used self-reflection and feedback from the directors. One director kept taking credit for my work. I stopped doing projects with him but never talked negatively about him. I was the one who needed to shine, not him. I wasn't going to let someone stab me in the back again."

I asked Denzel why get involved in office politics at all. He responded, "Office politics brings about power. When you're powerless, you can't stand up and do what's right."

Denzel's action steps

- ✓ Know which groups are favored by the boss.
- ✓ If meetings are going on without you, you're probably a jerk.
- ✓ Don't act arrogantly; confidence is acceptable.
- ✓ Don't take credit for other people's work; cooperation with a team is favored.
- ✓ Find out what skills and personality are needed to advance to the next level—highlight those skills.
- ✓ Choose projects that will gain you the spotlight in the stakeholder's eyes.
- ✓ Don't talk negatively about a supervisor.
- ✓ Office politics has a constructive role: it gives power for you to do the right thing.

Three top take-aways from Denzel

Office politics may be necessary to get the money, freedom, and time to do your best job.

Show your courage and confidence but don't come across as arrogant or conceited.

Showcase the talents, skills, and know-how that is needed to get to the next level.

III

Develop and show your intellect, emotional intelligence, and professional appearance

Leaders need to have three things to advance their career:
- Knowledge within their field.
- Emotional intelligence in dealing with people.
- An appropriate appearance and fitness level for the job.

Watching Oprah Winfrey helped Oliver move up the corporate ladder

"It's funny to say, but watching Oprah Winfrey on television gave me the tools to be where I am today." Oliver put both palms flat on his desk as if he was rooted in the company like a tree. "I started my corporate journey like most people—at the bottom. And like everyone, I wanted more. I was going to reach the top. So, I bought the executive presence books. The authors were vague:
'Be courageous.'
'Become a great public speaker.'
'You must have gravitas.'
'Dress nice.'

I kept asking myself, 'But how'?" He paused. "I didn't need books packed with statistics, '91% of CEOs have a background in accounting.' I don't have experience in accounting, and I still want to be the CEO. Tell me what to do—be specific. The only actionable advice I got from the books was how to dress. I changed my image to fit the job I wanted, but the other things were beyond my grasp, and some of the information was even wrong. I ended up hiring a life-coach who specialized in executive presence. Her name was Linda, and she was from Indianapolis, Indiana, so we met online. I started by telling Linda what I didn't want. 'I don't want you to tell me what's in the books—I've read them,' I said. 'I don't need wardrobe advice—I can look through a magazine. I need concrete guidance on how to act and what to do.'"

Oliver sat back in his chair and looked up at me. "In our first meeting, Linda gave me two pieces of advice. The first was: 'It's not about owning the room, it's about showing genuine interest in people around you. People like others who care for them. Instead of sending a text or email, talk with them. Prove you look out for the people next to you and sacrifice your time to make them feel safe, appreciated, even loved.' The advice was what I needed. I had concrete ideas to incorporate into my daily routine." Oliver stood up and walked to the front of his desk, leaning against a yellow and red amboyna burl desk.

"Do you know what the second piece of advice was?" he asked.

I shook my head, pen poised over my notebook.

"'Watch and emulate Oprah Winfrey.' How simple. I had seen her before but never spent the time to watch full episodes, until that evening. The first night, I watched three hours of Oprah's talk show reruns. I learned a lot. When she talked with people, she never looked rushed or bored. She gave them her full attention. She shared her setbacks and struggles, and in so doing, her guests opened up. Her feelings came across as authentic because she took what her subconscious felt and shared it. Oprah's empathy built trust in her guests. She was in tune with the person's needs—hugged them when they needed warmth and high-fived when she was proud."

Oliver pushed himself away from his desk and walked toward a table with a water pitcher and glasses. He slid a glass filled to the brim towards me, spilling a few drops on his immaculate desk.

He poured himself a second glass, then continued, "From my sessions with Linda, I learned that attitudes toward coworkers and employees matter more than position. Be tolerant and welcoming of each person's perspective. Let people feel free to express ideas without risk of embarrassment. If you don't, performance suffers, and turn-over increases." Oliver paused, taking a drink of water. "Being kind is hard, but worth it. Empathy makes you feel good. It's like eating healthy: harder than eating junk food, but you feel better for it. Connect with people. The easiest way to express empathy is to tell personal stories."

Oliver refilled his glass, shook his head and continued, "It sounds a bit silly for a man in an expensive suit, but I started acting like Oprah. A manly version, of course, but still Oprah." He puffed out his chest and sat up tall. "And, believe it or not, people responded. My coworkers started to help me with projects. One time a young lady spent her entire weekend running up a major project for our team. I asked her why she spent so much time and effort. Her response was, 'You would do the same for me.'"

Oliver smiled and tilted his head. "Do you want to hear an embarrassing story?"

I nodded eagerly.

"It's about how coworkers treated me after I started the Oprah technique," he said. "I've always loved singing, even as a kid. I'm part of a small band that gets together and makes music every week—just for fun. We volunteer to go to places, like retirement homes, to sing. That year, we had an important gig in the local town hall, so I practiced in the conference room, here in this building, which has great acoustics. I arrived early three times a week, went in there all by myself, and practiced for about forty minutes. I had done it for weeks, and this one time, I forgot the lines to a Beatles song. I paused, stumbling over my words. On the other side of the wall, I heard a female's voice pick up where I left off. Mortified, I clapped my hands over my mouth. To think she had been in the office early each day and had listened to me sing for weeks. Then I thought again. She wasn't trying to embarrass me. She was trying to help me remember the lines. I sent her a handwritten thank you note with a picture of a yellow submarine on it."

Oliver went into his desk drawer and pulled out a journal. "This is where I took notes during meetings. Not just corporate meetings. When I watched Oprah, I took notes here too. I can't give you my journal, but if you want to take a picture of the advice, I got from Oprah or write them down, feel free."

I pulled out my cell phone to take some pictures. Oliver only had three pages of notes from the coach.

Oliver's action steps

- ✓ When in a conversation, give your full attention, don't appear rushed or bored.
- ✓ Share your hardships to make yourself more approachable.
- ✓ Share how you're feeling and genuinely ask about the feelings of other people.
- ✓ Allow people to share their opinion without fear of embarrassment.
- ✓ Show your humanity by telling personal stories.

Notes from Oliver's executive coach

Make an extra effort to connect with your coworkers and the people who work for you.
- ✼ Instead of sending a text, visit the person in their office.
- ✼ If someone comes to you with a problem, take the time to listen.
- ✼ Don't interrupt your coworkers when they speak to you.
- ✼ At the end of every day, make a note of what happened and how the interactions went.

The next time someone asks for advice, listen to their problem and then share one of your own struggles. Seeing how you overcame your problem will motivate them to persevere and make them respect you even more, as they see how hard you worked to get to your current position.

When something embarrassing happens to a coworker or employee, reassure them and make them feel better. By showing empathy, you can create a permanent bond with them.

Jack hopped on a motorcycle and landed in another high-paying job

Jack and I walked along the Bahnhofstrasse. He was in a black suit and gleaming leather shoes. A tram full of people rumbled past us. I looked at the blue and white commuter train, seeing the familiar flag of Switzerland on its side. The tram was sliding through the middle of the street, flanked by high-end shops. Distracted, Jack bumped into a gentleman, smiled politely, and apologized.

"Kein problem," the stranger said. No problem.

Jack turned toward me and gestured toward an elegant shop front labeled 'Confiserie Bachmann.' "Let's go in here. It's my favorite bakery."

I followed him and inhaled deeply as the scent of hundreds of little chocolate pralines enveloped us.

"Wow." I stood, taking in the gleaming brown floors and walls, the bustling salespeople and the chairs in the shape of macaroons.

"Welcome to Switzerland," Jack said. "A different world."

I had flown in the day before to meet with Jack. As CEO of a big international firm, Jack was the epitome of executive presence. He had every box checked: he was confident but kind, a natural leader who wasn't afraid to listen to his employees, and a fantastic public speaker. But there was one thing that had brought him crashing down during a weak economy.

"I was calm during the storm," Jack said after we sat down and ordered. "I kept a level-head while others squealed. I could bring peace to a heated merger. Public speaking came easy for me. I cared for people, and they knew it. I could cheer up the most down-trodden of the lot. The one thing that brought me crashing down was my materialism."

I looked at the confident, well-dressed man in front of me and frowned. Where was this going?

"I wanted everything. If I didn't have it, I would earn a bonus and buy it. I negotiated expensive items into my contract so that the company would buy them for me. The mini-mansion I lived in and the Audi I drove were both perks of being a senior executive—paid for by the company. I filled both with marvelous things. For example, I bought a Critical Mass car stereo for the company car."

He paused as I took a bite out of my cheese sandwich. I chewed and gasped.

"Wow. What do they put in these things? This is the best sandwich of my life," I exclaimed.

He chuckled. "The secrets of the Swiss. Baked goods and cheese are the highest cultural goods here."

I finished chewing and looked up, pen hovering over my notebook. "Sorry, I interrupted you. Please go on."

"If I wasn't wearing Brioni, it was Tom Ford. Soon, my fast car wasn't enough—I needed a Ducati motorcycle. I looked the part; I was the part. That is until the economy went into a piranha tank. I wasn't the only one who lost his job. But it hit me hard. Besides my six-figure salary, I also lost the company house, the car, and even the stereo I put in the car. I had expenses and a reputation to uphold. Plus, my wife and I moved to Switzerland that year to be closer to her family. I kept spending money like I always had, even more, because we needed a place to live. Have you ever tried to live in the Four-Seasons?" Jack stopped, and I pictured him in an indoor pool doing laps at his hotel/home.

Jack picked up the dainty flower and vase, which formed the centerpiece of our table. "As I rode my Ducati to network with people in this new country, I soon realized the rules were different here. I showed up to my job interviews in my fancy suit, with a wristwatch that cost more than other people's cars. But the meetings never went well. The only feedback I got was I 'wasn't the right fit at this time' and 'didn't fit with the company's values.' I remember looking at myself in a full-length mirror one day, after yet another such meeting. That was the first time I noticed the problem: I looked like a tyrant."

He slicked back his hair and took a sip of his coffee. "I met an American friend here in Zurich. He'd been living in the country for several years and gave me some advice. 'The Swiss are different,' he told me. 'They are into understatement. They don't like show-offs'. The term shocked me. Had I become a show-off?"

Jack paused again. "I started re-evaluating my life and priorities. For a while, I had to restrain from spending all-together—until my desires became more reasonable. I realized my desires had been controlling me like a puppet: I wanted a Patek Phillipe, so I worked long hours to get the bonus. I changed. I downsized. I eliminated the clutter, and in so doing, the chaos in my mind vanished. I kept a few of the things I loved and could continue to use: my motorcycle, two suits, a nice watch, and all my shoes."

I glanced down again at his glistening leather shoes. "I guess you have to set priorities," I said.

"Exactly. My wife and I moved in with her parents, who didn't charge us rent, but we had to cook for them. I love cooking, so no big deal. I joined a motorcycle riding club, and that's how I ended up getting this job." Jack's hands pointed to his bike helmet. "I found an outside interest and made connections. The most balanced executive has outside interests. They put away the cell phone and stop thinking about work. Most of my peers play golf, but I know a few painters and one published author. They do something different, giving them a different perspective on their paid job." Jack pointed at me, then said, "You could bicycle, lay bricks, hunt, anything besides sitting and taking notes." He laughed, and I smiled.

Jack's laugh turned into a roar. "Oh, I just remembered this." He set down the vase with a bang. "I travel as a way for me to shut off from work. It's one of the things that keeps me sane while working a high-stress job, and every time I come back, I book another trip right away. That way, I have something to look forward to. I love going overseas or on a cruise because it means I can't connect during the vacation. Ever since I was a kid, I wanted to see the pyramids in Egypt. I wanted to go into a tomb and go back in history. In my early thirties, my wife and I finally took the trip. We flew into Cairo at 2:00 AM local time. The city was alive with people. There was a line to get haircuts. Grocery stores were open and busy. I asked the taxi driver why everyone was working like this, and he said it's the people's dream to give to their children more than their parents gave to them. I found out the Egyptians would work at several jobs, 12-15 hours each day. I began to think about my situation and how lucky I was to work in such an affluent part of the world."

Jack paused and looked back at the flower and vase, then refocused his attention on me. "During my trip, I hired a guide, and we both rode camels between historic sites. We went into burial tombs, and he interpreted the hieroglyphics. On my last day, we stopped for dinner in the shade of a pyramid—the desert was still boiling. I was exhausted and longing for a nice cold shower." Jack's eyes widened, and he sat up in his macaroon-shaped chair. "As I slumped against a boulder, I felt a cool breeze followed by a gentle rain. How refreshing! And what a great way to end my day. The shower covered me from head to toe, but when I looked up, I saw my guide snickering. There wasn't a cloud in the sky. I looked upwind and saw a camel urinating. His pee was blowing in the wind and drenching my left side. And you know what they say about having a camel bladder."

We were still laughing when the waitress came with the bill.

"That will be thirty-four francs fifty."

I gasped. "Thirty-five dollars for two sandwiches, cookies, and coffees?" I whispered to Jack.

"Welcome to Switzerland," he said. "You've finally arrived. Also, because I knew you were flying in to see me. I wrote a few things down. To be honest, I didn't want you to feel like it was a wasted trip. I also didn't want to forget anything important." Jack pulled out a piece of folded paper from his front left pocket and handed it to me. Typed on the paper were Jack's notes.

Jack's action steps

- ✓ Stay calm, especially while others panic.
- ✓ Use your tone, words, and body language to calm people down.
- ✓ Show you care with your words and actions.
- ✓ Find ways to be happy, through activities, without buying new things.
- ✓ Focus your purchases on a few beautiful items that bring you joy.
- ✓ Remove clutter—streamline your environment.
- ✓ Don't let your wants control you. Instead, showcase restraint.
- ✓ Have outside interests in which you leave work behind.

Jack's notes

Examine your material desires.
- ☙ Each time you feel the desire to buy something, examine the reason. Why do you want to buy it? Is it because of a genuine need, or is it related to your social status?
- ☙ Decide on 2-3 'splurge' areas in your life and eliminate the others. You may have a high-paying job now, but the future is insecure, and it's better to have a safety cushion.

Start or cultivate an interest unrelated to your work.
- ✣ If you already have an outside interest, spend 2-3 hours a week on it. If you don't, think back on some hobbies you loved as a child. Possibly a sport, art, or culture related. Is there a way for you to pick it back up or start something similar?

Take a trip to a less affluent country.
- ✣ From now on, take regular vacations to shut off from work, starting with a trip to a third-world country. While there, observe the culture, work ethic, and values of the locals. What is their perspective? What can you learn from them?

Knowing his clients' goals gave Liam a competitive edge

"When you called, you said you wanted to learn my inside secrets to success."

Liam was shorter and heavier than I expected. He nodded his short-cropped head towards his spotless desk, where a Montblanc skeleton blue hour fountain pen, a pad of fine paper, and a laptop rested.

'Wow, I wonder what his cupboards look like,' I thought. I envisioned drawers neatly stacked with thousands of files, color-coded, and organized. Or - maybe it was all just a façade. What if the empty desk was just an act and his drawers were full of jumbled up, messy papers?

"Are you okay?" Liam asked, and I jumped, realizing I'd been staring at his desk drawer for the last two minutes.

He handed me a piece of the thick paper and his fountain pen. "List your top 12 stakeholders, supervisors, clients. Next to their names, write their goals," he demanded.

I began to write but only came up with three, and one of those was my mother. Liam took my paper and scanned it.

"You must learn to predict what your stakeholders want." He looked me in the eyes, and I lowered my gaze.

"My biggest secret is knowing who I'm in business for and what they want," he continued. "Every one of my corporate leaders can write down their top 12 constituents. They can also express the top customers' goals and what each wants.

Knowing them by name, their goals, and being able to predict what they want is the reason for our success."

Liam adjusted the thick stationery on his desk, so it aligned perfectly with the edge of the table.

He raised two fingers and continued, "Our second reason we're successful is that we take feedback seriously. It is our opportunity to grow—no need to get defensive or blame others. Take responsibility. Take it seriously. Those people who can't take feedback and grow are cut loose."

He paused and linked his fingers together, staring into the distance. "We don't fire them immediately. We wait until they stumble on their next project. They will stumble because they didn't take their supervisor's advice and feedback. You see, winners are bold and stand out. When bad things happen, the best are honest and take responsibility. Put your attention on what needs to be accomplished and stop worrying about the things that won't help. We use feedback to make improvements. Each adjustment brings you one step higher on your corporate ladder."

Liam held out his hand and pointed to his shiny wedding ring with one diamond inlaid in the center. "Have you ever seen an uncut diamond? It's dull, lifeless," he said. "Feedback is like cutting facets in a gemstone—each new facet creates more brilliance and sparkle. Someone who doesn't grow from their failures is like an uncut diamond."

He withdrew his hand, and I went back to my notes. "You learn from each attempt and fail when you do nothing," he said. "We care less about your failure compared to your growth from it."

Liam slid his hands over his nearly empty desk and opened and closed the cap of his pen. "Now, our feedback model: praise in public, reprimand in private." His hand hovered above his desk drawer.

I sat forward in my chair and held my breath. Would I get to see what was inside the drawer? But he withdrew his hand, and I hastily averted my gaze.

"We encourage, as part of our feedback model, 20% humility, and 80% self-advocacy. Our leaders always give credit where it's due—that's 20%. With the other 80%, they show how they bring value to the company by explaining how they've managed crises, took calculated risks, and earned money for the company."

Liam's cell phone rang. "Excuse me. I have to take this. One second." He stepped outside.

He came back into the office. "I'm sorry, Jim. I have to cut our meeting short. I know you came a long way to talk with me. I hope you got something out of our short time together." Liam walked me to the door and got back on his phone as I left.

Liam's action steps

- ✓ Be able to list your top 12 clients, their goals, and how you can help each one.
- ✓ When your attempt fails, ask yourself why and make sure to learn something. Never repeat your failures!
- ✓ Use feedback as an opportunity to grow.
- ✓ While getting feedback, don't get defensive or blame others; take responsibility and use it to make improvements.
- ✓ Praise in public, reprimand in private.
- ✓ Practice 80% self-promotion—tell the right people what you can offer; 20% humility—give credit where it's due.
- ✓ Be a risk-taker with fearless dominance, crisis management, and persuasiveness.

Liam's top three

Make a list of your uppermost 12 stakeholders, supervisors, or clients. For each one, list their:

- ❧ Primary goal(s)
- ❧ Reason they need you
- ❧ 2-3 best ways you can help them

The next time you get negative feedback, write it down. If you feel yourself getting defensive, sleep on it, and revisit your notes the next day. Implement the person's suggestions and observe what kind of difference it makes in your life.

When you have your next performance review, spend 80% of your time advocating for yourself and 20% of the time giving credit to everybody who helped you to get there.

Joyce's night-shift workers do all the labor

Joyce had picked me up from my hotel, and we drove toward the first bat house. "Joyce, thanks for meeting me. I'm interested in learning how you hire."

"I tell human resources I'm looking for employees who are self-motivated, work well in teams, and supportive of the company's vision." It wasn't a long ride. We reached a parking lot near a neighborhood pond. "I tell new employees our vision: 'Reduce bug populations naturally with bats to make human lives better.' Then I ask potential hires. What can you do to help us reach this goal? I hire those who are passionate about what we do and are at the top 10% in their field."

We got out of her car and approached the pond. I added to what Joyce was saying. "Hire individuals who believe in your vision and want to make a difference. Those who are in for the money may be smart but won't put in as much dedication."

We reached the pond and started walking along the edge. A pole with bushes around it and a brown box on top came into focus. Joyce pointed toward the structure. "This is one of our bat houses. Notice the size. This house can hold over 100 bats. Each bat can eat about 8,000 insects in a night." Joyce went up to the bushes.

Joyce touched the red and green bush. "We like to use bushes that require high nitrogen content. The bat guano that drops from the houses feeds the foliage. This bush is a firethorn. People and animals don't want to get tangled in this type of plant. The plant helps protect our bats from animals looking for a meal and teenagers wanting to shake the pole to see what happens." I could see what looked like white bird poop on the plant near the pole.

"This bat house probably has about 20 bats living in it. We place our houses near water because that's where bats like to live." Joyce explained.

I took a look at the thorns of the bush and wondered if they were poisonous. "You mentioned hiring people. Tell me about forming your management team."

Joyce shook her head and walked to the far side of the bush. "When I started this company, I wanted diversity in thought."

I interrupted and added, "I've heard that diversity is important, and companies should hire a variety of ethnic backgrounds and different ages too."

"That's where corporate culture has it wrong." Joyce snapped. "Hiring someone because of the color of their skin works against what you want to accomplish. When people learn the hiring decision was made in part because of their color or sex, they become demotivated. They feel as if they are a token and there as a symbol representing diversity and not there for what they can contribute. Hiring for the diversity of thought is what corporate cultures need to focus upon." Joyce's tone seemed passionate about the subject.

Joyce continued, "The first step for hiring cognitively diverse people is first learn and be aware of your biases. Taking a bias test can be eye-opening as to the type of people you gravitate toward. I will tell you age is an easy one to see. Take me, for example. I'm not a baby bat pup, and I don't think like a millennial. Because I'm not young is why I have two boards."

"What do you mean? You have two boards of directors?" I asked.

"I have a team designed to gather information, build relationships, and speak on my behalf. Most importantly, this first team provide opposing views, new ideas, and are willing to tell me 'no.' They also decide on the timing of when to release information. I need diversity to see all aspects of the situation. I have Kristofer who is our perfectionist. Merlin is all about speed and getting things done quickly. Elizabeth is logical. Ronald is our debater and plays devil's advocate. Caryn, the commander, takes charge and gives orders. Teams are good at generating ideas, but someone needs to be in charge to make final decisions and set direction and give resources—Caryn is our woman. Finally, Elaine is our adventurer. She will gladly travel and arrange locals to set up the bat houses to our specifications."

"Then what are you saying about having two teams?" I asked.

Joyce responded, "The second board is a shadow board of younger people, again a cognitively diverse group. Two reasons we have the shadow is to mentor them to take over the company and keep our legacy alive—how we do business based upon our values. The second reason, older people don't think like younger people. Younger people know what to say on social media. I would say something like, 'bats eat bugs.' The shadow group would put out, 'save your loved ones from disease and let bats eat the insects that carry death.' You can tell one is much more effective." We reached Joyce's car, and we got in heading to check out another bat house.

As we were driving, Joyce continued, "In these two groups, we want those who have experience—proven. We also need younger people who are hungry to make a difference in the world. We don't want arrogant people. 'Confidence without attitude' is what we need."

"It appears you have everything perfectly set up," I said.

"No, we aren't perfect. We make lots of mistakes," Joyce replied. "Past failures are ok. They're learning experiences." Joyce pulled the car over and pulled out a tablet. "At first, we only wanted to hire those people who had the right image to represent our company. Image is important, but people need to possess so much more." Joyce handed me the tablet. "Here is a list we came up with of the traits that are important for future hires."

I asked if I could take a picture of the list and share it. Joyce indicated it wouldn't be an issue.

Future employees:

- Focus upon self-improvement—deep learning.
- Have strong communication skills—verbal, written, and body language.
- Confidence in their field.
- No whiners or complainers.
- Practices gratitude for their accomplishments, possessions, and position.
- Keeps promises.
- Helps other people.
- Listens instead of directs.
- Lets go of control—isn't a control freak.

After I took the picture, Joyce started to drive again. "As I was saying, we've done things wrong in the past. What we look at is what did we do right as well as wrong? What can we change? We pull advice from experts in the field and trust our gut. It's called intuitive leadership." Joyce pulled up to the next lake. I could see her bat house a short walk away.

As we got out of the car, Joyce continued, "We encourage our top leaders not to solve every problem. We want the juniors in our organization to learn for themselves. If a team comes up with a plan and the leader intuitively knows it's less than 50% right, she'll send them back to brainstorming. If the team has it 50-60% right, the leader will ask questions to encourage them to come to the right and final decision. Finally, when the team gets it at least 70% right, the leader lets them run with it. Possibly fail, but learn from their mistakes. The one thing people ask is, 'What are the true risks.' We develop leaders by focusing on developing confidence in the employees. We base our future upon setting a foundation of people who can solve problems for themselves. The bottom line, leaders don't answer questions but ask questions for rising leaders to learn and grow. We don't come across as 'know it all's.'" Joyce touched the leaves of the shrub under the bat house. The bush was different, and the bat house was more substantial.

"Do you only deal with bat houses?" I asked.

"We're now designing bridges over waterways for rural areas designed to house bats underneath. We have to be careful about the design. Bridges require maintenance. No one wants to stick their hands up into a colony of bats. The bolts have to be in areas that don't get covered in guano and are accessible," Joyce said.

"How can designing bridges for bats and putting up bat houses be profitable? It seems like people wouldn't be willing to pay for things that happen naturally." I half asked, and half stated.

"Let me take a step back and explain the profitability of this organization." Joyce started to walk away from the bat house and back toward the parking lot. "You wouldn't think bat houses would have a high total addressable market, which is called TAM. But if you look at the larger industry of bug control, it is well over the $20 billion thresholds we look for before jumping into a new venture. When you add in the disease control aspect, we are number one in our industry."

I put out my hand like I needed her to pause. I then asked, "Why such a large amount for the threshold?"

"Most corporations follow this same guideline," Joyce said. "They look at the TAM and plan on capturing 5% of the business; that would be worth $1 billion. Below that dollar amount, it's not worth it."

"I didn't realize bats were so profitable. It's also great you have these furry creatures working the night shift for you." I laughed at my joke.

"Right, if you count the bats as employees, were one of the largest employers in the world." Joyce snickered as she said it. "Speaking of the world, we were recently called to set up bat houses in Costa Rica to help with the dengue fever epidemic. We used native bats to start the populations of our new bat houses. The cameras we have set up indicate the bats are breeding and populations are increasing."

"How did you manage to get into the multi-national arena?" I asked.

"From day one, we've been a world organization," Joyce responded. "We are so successful because we celebrate projects of the month, not an employee of the month. When you celebrate just one person, you have many losers and one winner. In contrast, when we celebrate a project, the entire team feels the positive feedback. Speaking of feedback, people require positive feedback based on their strengths and professional competencies 35 times a year to feel fulfilled at work."

"How do you have time to give that much feedback?"

"It doesn't all have to come from the boss. It can come from coworkers as well. One of our top team members wrote a book about bats. It was well written and informative. This person desires kudos for her professional know-how. To make this happen, I bought one of her books for every employee," Joyce said. I smiled at Joyce's generosity and thoughtfulness.

Joyce gave me a ride back to my hotel. Before I left, she gave me a gift certificate for a bat house of my very own. With the value, I ordered a large one and had it delivered. I followed the directions about how high to hang it and which direction it should face, based upon my climate.

Joyce's action steps

- ✓ Hire self-motivated people, who work well in teams, and are supportive of the company's vision.
- ✓ Form your team of decision-makers with a diversity of cognitive thought.
- ✓ Form a secondary board with younger people to train them up and get their perspective.
- ✓ Empower your decision-making team to decide on the timing of initiatives, voice their opposing views, come up with new ideas, and be willing to say 'no.'
- ✓ Allow for mistakes to be made—mistakes are learning experiences.
- ✓ Base new ventures on $20 million + Total Addressable Market.
- ✓ Celebrate the people who do well with a successful project.
- ✓ Organize feedback models, so each employee receives 35+ positive feedback examples based upon what they value: their strengths and professional virtues.

Joyce's top three

Hire a cognitively diverse team of decision-makers.
- ↣ Self-motivated.
- ↣ Work well in teams.
- ↣ Supportive of the company's vision.
- ↣ Include younger people to train them up and get their perspective.

Don't be a micromanager.
- ↣ Allow for mistakes to be made.
- ↣ Guide teams by asking questions to train them to make decisions on their own.

Celebrate successes with feedback based on the employee's values.

Mindy created a personal brand that propelled her to the top

'Thomas Tucker Training.' I squinted at the violently purple sign, then pushed the door open and entered the LED-lit space. A classic rock song was playing on the stereo, and I immediately felt energized, ready to move. 'Maybe I need to start going to a gym,' I thought.

Across the room, a petite woman lay on the bench, holding an Olympic bar with more weight than most men could lift. Trainer Thomas stood behind her, spotting, as she blasted through five reps. Each time the weight was high, she took a big gulp of air, then held her breath until the bar was going back up again.

Thomas turned around and smiled at me. "Ah, Mindy, your guest is here," he said.

Mindy looked up at me and wiped the sweat from her forehead.

"Welcome," she said. "I'm so glad you could make it. I have two exercises to go, but we can talk as I work."

She sat up on the bench. "Health equals attractiveness. People want to work with and be with confident, healthy people. Before I met Thomas, I had most of the attributes of a successful executive, but I felt self-conscious about the way I looked. Starting regular workouts and a meal plan has helped me to feel more confident and self-assured."

Thomas helped Mindy to get the bar off and then back on the rack. He turned his head and said, "Mindy already had a lot going for her. She cared for people, and her communication was concise and articulate. Poised under pressure and decisive was Mindy's strengths. But she wasn't happy with her weight. Her lack of self-confidence caused her professional problems."

Thomas turned to Mindy and gestured towards a mat on the floor, where another heavy bar sat. "Move over to the dead-lift next." He paused and turned towards me. "You know how people are their worst critic?" I nodded in agreement.

"Mindy wasn't ugly," Thomas continued. "She wasn't overweight. She only thought she was. If you ask me, she was perfect before. At first, I didn't even know why she wanted to hire me. But with my workout and the diet we put her on, she lost fat and gained muscle."

"That's great!" I said, watching Mindy complete perfect dead-lifts on her mat. I wouldn't have been able to do one at that weight.

After completing her five reps, Mindy lay back down on the mat and exhaled.

"To optimize my health, I get seven to eight hours of sleep every night," she said. "I used to work late at night, eating sugary snacks to stay awake. But since implementing a regular bedtime as Thomas told me to, I get more work done in less time." She beamed. "I feel less stressed, and my sugar cravings have disappeared."

Thomas laughed. "I guess I'm worth the expense, after all."

Mindy sat up and reached forwarded to stretch her hamstrings. "You did wonders for me and my image in the corporate world, Thomas." She looked me in the eyes. "The only thing he couldn't help me with was my wardrobe. Look at him—muscle shirt with the sides cut out. Pants that look like they belong in a 1980's music video. Works great for the studio, but not so much in the corporate world."

Thomas grimaced at her, but Mindy ignored him and continued. "See the color of my top?" She gestured to her mint green workout shirt. "This color is my brand—my signature style. It's a small eccentric that differentiates me and has become part of my reputation. I could have used a personality quirk, but I already have plenty of personalities. I lacked the executive look. But when I started training with Thomas, I felt better about my body. Every week, I could see improvement, and this motivated me to focus on my appearance in other ways as well. I started dressing for the job promotion I wanted every day. Other people wore jeans on Friday, not me. I kept a consistent, professional look. Nothing about my appearance distracted from the impression I wanted to give. If someone asked why I didn't dress down on casual Friday, I told them I had an important meeting." She brushed some lint off her workout pants and continued. "I also started to wear different kinds of make-up for different purposes. When I want to emphasize my honesty and integrity, I wear only a little mascara and powder. But when I want to appear confident and in control, I ramp it up and wear more dramatic make-up."

Thomas directed Mindy to the next exercise—barbell row.

"Mindy was very diligent and followed my plan to the letter. We focused on low carbohydrate intake and weight-bearing exercise. She kept to a workout schedule and never deviated." Thomas looked up at me. "Remember the ice storm three months ago? Mindy called me, saying she can't come to my gym because of the weather. She insisted we do her workout virtually. She had some basic equipment at her home. I improvised, using more bodyweight exercises for her that morning."

Mindy moved to the overhead press and said, "I follow Thomas' advice. Now, I go heavy in all my lifts. But we didn't start heavy. Thomas had me start with the bar and no added weight." Mindy shot Thomas a dirty look.
"He called it 'a beginners' exercise for women', which made me want to try even harder if only to show him how strong women can be. But he was right, that's as much as I could lift. Since then, I've been coming three times a week, and we were able to increase the weight five pounds a week."

"These days, Mindy is stronger than many of my male clients," Thomas said. "I had Mindy here lifting five exercises, alternating between heavier and lighter weights for optimal muscle gain. She was sore after every session, but she kept coming back for more."

"What are the exercises you gave her?" I asked, thinking of my home gym. Maybe I could spend more time there.

"I made sure the exercise plan was balanced," Thomas explained. "The squat and dead-lift focused on her largest muscles. Growing these helped her burn more calories, even while in meetings. The overhead press and bench-press developed her upper body. Those gave her that toned look you see today. Finally, the barbell row balanced her muscles to improve her posture—keeps her from being a frumpy sloucher." Thomas gave Mindy a one-two punch in the arm.

I smiled and leaned my notebook against a wall to make quick notes.

"Still to this day, we stick to those five exercises," Mindy explained. "Thomas also created a meal plan for me. It was strict. He only allowed me to eat carbohydrates one time a month. Other than that, I had to keep them low. He also limited how much protein I was going to consume at each meal. The weirdest part of this diet was the amount of fat. I ate plenty of good fats like avocados, coconut oil, and olive oil, but I avoided most of the salad dressings because of the soybean or canola oil."

"Don't forget about the types of meats," Thomas interrupted. He turned towards me. "She could occasionally have red meat and limited her chicken and other meats raised on soy products or hormones. Her diet was a lot of wild-caught fish and eggs."

"At the beginning, I lived for my monthly cheat day," Mindy sighed. "In February, it was Valentine's Day, and in April, I had to wine and dine a client."

"Do you schedule your cheat days? What if there's a spontaneous party or client meeting?" I asked.

"Yeah, I schedule out which day each month I'll break the diet. My clients and friends understand, and there are plenty of alternatives I can order. At first, I would go hog-wild on my cheat days, but now I have a few things I've missed and enjoy. Taking probiotic pearls with L. gasseri and L. rhamnosus and cutting out the artificial sweeteners helped. Those sweeteners bring about cravings later in the day and wreak havoc on your gut. Best to just cut them out."

"Yeah, remember what else wreaks havoc on your gut—nightshades," Thomas exclaimed as Mindy started her final set of barbell rows. "Mindy spoke to me about her digestive problems, and I suspected she had a leaky gut. I told her to avoid tomatoes, eggplant, peanuts, beans, and peppers and increase her salt intake. She adds salt to everything. It helps her get over the brain fog people have as they begin this diet. Salt in her coffee, water, and meals." Thomas chuckled and moved Mindy over to the mat.

Mindy pointed to her legs and said, "Look at me. I can lift more weight than you can, and am I too big? Am I some muscle-bound gym freak? No—I look toned and in shape." She looked to the door as a tall, young man entered, dressed in a white gym outfit.

"I'm still lady-like. It's a big misconception that lifting weights makes you big. In reality, it helps you to look toned and lean. Of course, you can train to get ripped. I've seen some of Thomas' male clients: six-pack abs and biceps you can't get two hands around." Mindy gazed over at the next client, who was taking off his jacket. She stepped back into a calf stretch and exhaled.

"That's all the time we've got," Thomas said. "Mindy, I'll see you on Friday."

Mindy smiled at me as she switched legs and turned to me. "I hope this helped. Call again if you need any other advice."

"I might just stay and sign up myself. Bigger biceps might help me open up those pickle jars," I said.

Mindy's action steps

- ✓ Focus on getting healthier to become more attractive.
- ✓ Get 7-8 hours of sleep.
- ✓ Present yourself as a healthy, proactive individual to build up your brand.
- ✓ Use a small eccentric element to differentiate yourself—something you wear, a personality trait, or a hairstyle.
- ✓ Don't wear anything that could distract from the impression you want to create.
- ✓ Ladies can put on dramatic makeup to look confident and in control or minimal makeup to give the impression of honesty.
- ✓ Consistently wear clean, attractive, modern clothing for the job you want and works well for your body shape.
- ✓ Find a diet you can stick with to create the physique you want.
- ✓ Create a workout routine to become physically fit.
- ✓ Keep to your workout schedule.

Mindy and Thomas' favorite three

Experiment with getting more sleep.
- Go to bed early enough to get 7-8 hours of sleep.
- Take note of any changes in your energy levels.

Find an exercise routine and a diet that helps you stay in shape.

Find a color or accessory to set you apart from everybody else.

A dog saved Bethany's life and taught her how to lead

I boarded a red and glass box tied to cables headed for the Summit House Restaurant in Washington State. I was alone, and the cabin could've fit four people. I was to meet Bethany at the top. Bethany started her own company and was successful. I was looking forward to meeting her and also the views from the outdoor seating. Lucky for me, it was summertime at this mountain resort.

As I reached the top, I could see a building. Half was dark brown, and the other part was made of stacked stone. A second building was white and looked modern—raised off the ground and covered in windows. I scanned the area looking for Bethany, figuring I would notice her from her social media presence. She was sitting at a glossed picnic bench with a green umbrella. She was looking toward Mount Ranier. "Bethany," I called out as I walked toward her. "Thanks for meeting me."

Bethany stood and shook my hand. I knew she was tall, but she almost had me beat. "Isn't this a beautiful spot?"

"It's breathtaking. I feel a bit short of breath being up this high."

"Here have a seat. I ordered a glass of wine for myself. Our waitress is Vivian. She'll be back in a few minutes. Hey, and don't be surprised if our order takes a while. People come here for the view, not the quick service."

I sat down and scanned the other tables to see what they were eating and drinking. I noticed a hamburger with an egg on top. That looked as good as the snow-capped mountain views. "Bethany, I wanted to talk with you about how you formed your own company and what gave you the courage to make it happen."

Bethany pointed over to Mount Ranier. "That mountain over there changed me." She paused and shook her head like she needed to start from the beginning. "I have a background as a sleep scientist. Before my life-changing hike, I was working for a sleep lab in Seattle. I've always loved helping people, but this place simply got 'em in and out. Monitor their sleep and sell the fat people a $2,000 CPAP machine."

"That sounds terrible," I responded. "Tell me about this hike."

"I wasn't going to climb to the top. I was just going out for the day with my dog. I packed a lunch and a bunch of water into my usual day-pack. We set out early on a trail that was barely used. I let Steve, my dog, off his leash and let him run. He's a good boy who stays close to me but has to sniff every tree along the path. It's easier to keep a steady pace without his leash." Bethany pulled out her phone and showed me a photo of Steve.

"That's a good-looking dog."

"Thanks. That dog saved my life on that hike. We got to a part of the trail that was narrow. A steep bank was on my left. Instead of stepping over a root, I stepped on it. It was slippery. I lost my footing and tumbled down the hill. During the fall, I fractured my fibula."

"Oh, no!" I exclaimed. "No one was with you?"

"Just my dog and me. Here I was at the bottom of this ravine. Steve came bouncing down the hill like this was part of the hike. I could tell my leg was broken and knew I had to find a way back to civilization as quickly as possible. If I followed the path, it would take too long on a broken leg. I also knew no one was going to be on that path any time soon. And I wasn't expected home until after nightfall. So no one would start looking for me until late that night."

"What did you do?"

"I started by making a splint for my leg with some sticks and straps. I cut a branch I could use for support. After I felt I was ready to move, I rummaged through my bag to figure out what I could use. I found a map. I studied the map, not remembering where I last used it. Looking around, I realized this was a map of the area I was laying."

"That's great. You could use that to get yourself out."

Bethany scoffed, "That's what I thought too. But it was the wrong map. Torn up and me not paying enough attention, I was looking at trails of Mount Baker."

"Oh my gosh, you used the wrong map?"

"Yeah, I plotted a course that would take me directly from where I thought I was to a road where I could flag down a car. I skipped lunch, knowing I wouldn't make it to the road until nightfall. I was moving slow. Steve kept my encouragement up by running back and forth, checking on me." Our waitress, Vivian, brought me the Ranier Burger with the egg on top. Bethany got a salad.

"This burger is good. But back to your story. What happened?"

"Night started to come, and I kept at it. I knew the road must be close. As it got darker, it got too dangerous to walk and slide down the hills. It also started to get cold. I called for Steve and pushed my body under the roots of a fallen tree. My dog snuggled me to keep me warm."

"That's amazing. What a great pet."

"Not only that, but he also didn't sleep at all that night. He kept watch. Anytime an animal started to approach, Steve would bark and scare it off. He protected me from being attacked. That night, I knew coyotes were walking near us, and I could hear wolves in the distance."

"Were you scared?"

Bethany nodded, and her eyes got wide, "Yes. I was petrified. But Steve was there to protect me. I didn't sleep well, but I did doze off and on that night. I got enough rest that by dawn, we could continue." Bethany held up her cell phone. "Every hour, I would turn my cell phone on and check for a signal. I learned the hard way. Leaving it on with no signal drains the battery."

"Near 11:00 AM, I could hear people shouting, 'Bethany, Steve!' I was too exhausted to shout very loud, but Steve's bark made it through the trees. Three friends came running through the woods toward us. One had a radio and was yelling into it, 'We've found them.' They did find us, thanks to my dog, Steve."

"I can't believe they found you off the trail."

"Me either. My friends helped me get to a hospital for treatment. I didn't realize how badly I was banged up. I knew about my leg, but I was bruised and cut in all sorts of places. Steve, on the other hand, slept for 5 hours, and he was his old self again." Bethany got fixated on the words she just spoke and sat silently. I didn't interrupt.

She then continued, "That accident and what I learned shaped my decisions and how I would run my company. I quit my job and started my sleep practice. We would take the lessons I learned on Mount Ranier and incorporate them into our daily practice. Steve taught me to be protective of the ones I love. Protect your employees from harm."

Bethany continued, as I wrote. "Remember the map? Even if you don't know where you're going, move forward. Without a direction, hope is lost. For success, you need a sense of direction. You have to take calculated risks—have and show courage. Even if the direction is wrong, it's better to have hope than lay down and give up. Following that map gave me a direction to move. Now, don't get me wrong. I don't need you telling people to run their business into the ground."

I interrupted slightly, "It's like a teenager. If he has an idea of what he wants to become, he'll have the motivation and go to school to make it happen. Those who are clueless just meander around and look lost."

Bethany shook her head. "Right. A teen can change their mind. He could decide to be a teacher today, and then while in college, decide petroleum engineers make more money."

Bethany changed subjects and pointed to my journal. "Our meetings are with presence. I remove distractions. No phones are allowed. To prevent the problems hunger brings, I always have healthy snacks. During the meetings, we encourage our employees to slow down and reduce stress. When these things are combined, our communication improves. Besides, an executive who appears tired and stressed doesn't need more responsibilities of high-stakes projects."

I added, "Getting involved in those projects that have visibility is a sure-fire way to advance."

"My company is small. I'm more interested in making the right decisions. When we're at a crossroads, everyone makes their mind up during their prime-time. My prime-time is in the morning. My assistant, who helps make major decisions, functions best late at night. Two other employees seem to get their best work done mid-morning. So after we meet, we think about our obstacles and reconvene after everyone has had their prime-time to think about the change. Impulse decision can be detrimental."

"I see. Your impulse decision to follow the wrong map was detrimental as well."

Bethany smirked. "Yeah, I guess you're right, Jim."

"Bethany, how is your sleep practice different than the one you came from?"

"We tell people the truth and give it to them in writing." Bethany pulled up a file on her phone and showed it to me. "There are three levels to improve sleep. If you're having trouble sleeping, you must incorporate the first level right away. Typically, those changes are enough to overcome most people's troubles. If those aren't enough, we move them onto the next level. The last level could be of benefit but are still unproven."

"Do you mind if I take a picture of these?"

"No, I'll just send them to you. You can share the list however you want."

I looked Bethany in the eye to see if she was serious. "Thanks. These will be helpful. A lot of people suffer from poor sleep."

"I know. Those people who consistently get four hours of sleep or less per night are at an increased risk of coming down with type 2 diabetes. Also, they can't focus. It's as if they're drunk. At a minimum, people need five hours of sleep, and that's just to stay alive. That's if those five hours are quality, restorative sleep. Most people need seven to eight because they spend most of their sleep time in states that aren't restorative. The number one problem is alcohol. People think that it helps them sleep, and it does help them fall asleep but not the right type of sleep, and then when the buzz wears off, they wake up."

"I've heard that before. I use a fan to drown out some outside noises."

"A fan is good, and some are considered pink noise, like rain or a heartbeat. Pink noise gets you into slow-wave sleep. That level of sleep is best for memory formation and burning fat. That's on our second list because not everyone needs ambient noise." Vivian dropped off the check, and Bethany paid for our meals.

Together, we rode the lift back to the parking lot. I thanked Bethany for her time and the story of how a dog saved her life and helped form her new company.

Bethany's action steps

- ✓ Protect your employees. Show them you value them and their wellbeing.
- ✓ Have meetings with presence to improve communication—remove distractions: phones, hunger, sleepiness, and stress.
- ✓ Eliminate impulse decisions—let employees make major decisions during their prime-time.

- ✓ Get quality sleep. Minimum of 5 quality hours of sleep, but most people need 7-8 hours.
- ✓ Don't compromise your health for making a profit for the company. Don't insist your employees destroy their health for potential profit.
- ✓ Take calculated risks to show courage and give your professional life a sense of direction.

How to get the best night's sleep

Must-haves for quality sleep:
- Exercise for at least 30 minutes every day but not before bedtime.
- Don't go to bed drunk or buzzed. Avoid sleeping pills.
- Balance when you drink water. Hydrate, but not so much you have to go to the bathroom in the middle of the night.
- Keep your bed for only sex and sleep. Create a sleep sanctuary—a designated area.
- Install blackout curtains in your bedroom. Cover, or point your clock away to prevent any light reaching you.
- Go to bed at the same time each night—within 30 minutes. Preferably going to bed early and getting up early. Gradually make the change to an earlier bedtime.
- Skip caffeine within six hours of bed.
- Stop using nicotine. When it wears off, you wake up.
- Don't nap during the day.
- Use a comfortable mattress and pillow.

Will probably aid you getting a better night's sleep:
- Don't read or watch television in bed.
- Use magnesium cream on your skin before bed.
- Turn down the temperature in the room—68 degrees is a suitable starting temperature. Dropping down to 60 degrees could help.
- Recap your day, think about problems, and what you'll do tomorrow outside of bed in a designated spot and time. Having a negative connotation with your mattress, like work or restlessness, will further frustrate your inability to sleep.
- Take a teaspoon of coconut oil just before bed.
- Remove electronics from the room.
- Use white noise or better yet pink noise to drown out disturbances.
- Don't eat 4 hours before sleep.
- Try a low carb or ketogenic diet.
- Use a bedtime routine to get your mind focused on sleeping and follow the guidelines.

Could help you feel more rested the following morning:

- Shower before sleep, cold or lukewarm.
- Don't point head to the north or northern hemisphere. Align your head toward the east works well.
- Don't use snooze; set your alarm for the latest possible time.
- In the morning, expose as much skin (as appropriate) to the morning sun.
- Get as much sunlight during the day as possible.
- Don't lay in bed, unable to sleep. Lay down when you're sleepy.
- Avoid house lights, computers, and phones for one hour before bedtime. Use candles or lanterns to help avoid house lights.

Ben's formal schooling was online videos and reading in his parents' house

"I know my grandmother wanted me to use the graduation gift for college, but I didn't. In all honesty, it wouldn't have been enough anyway." Ben's voice echoed around the lobby of a high-rise in New York City. Despite his elegant suit, he looked almost too young to work in such a prestigious environment.

I let my gaze sweep around the ample space, tilting my head backward to take in the tall ceiling and the ornamental trees growing inside. The security guard at the main desk checked formally dressed office workers in and out in muted tones. We sat on a bench near one of the trees and could hear the water splashing into a large marble fountain at the center of the hall.

"Think about what people learn in college," Ben continued. "Do they take that knowledge from job to job? No, they learn on the job and advance their career by showcasing those skills to their supervisors or other businesses. How else could the CEO of a manufacturing company become the CEO of a finance company? It comes down to the skills he learned—his writing and management of people."

Ben paused and looked around at the endless stream of tailored suits, shiny heels, and expensive dresses streaming in and out of the building. "Many people go the college route, but it just didn't seem like the right path for me. I always wanted to be a trader, so I decided to skip college and learn how to trade stocks instead. It turns out, I didn't need a finance degree to make a 115% annual return on my grandmother's money."

"Wow," I said. "That's amazing."

"It is, but I worked hard for it. You have to know the jargon to advance. While others take four years to learn this in college, I spent a few months reading LinkedIn articles, finance blogs, and ebooks. I used online learning to become a swing trader. Now, I'm working for a company, controlling millions of dollars, and making even more money." Ben smiled at his success.

"At the start, there was a near-impossible list of skills and information I needed to learn. I was penniless, living with my parents, and had no job, but I was passionate about making money in the stock market. I knew that I would fail if I tried to change too much at once. So, I broke the goal up into manageable chunks and started waking up early to learn. Before my parents even thought about getting out of bed, I was up watching videos and reading. All of my learning was project-based and immersive: I learned by doing. Every night, I set myself goals for the next morning's session and prepared a glass of water with lemon juice, apple cider vinegar, and salt to wake me up."

I pulled a face, and Ben laughed.

"I know it sounds disgusting. But it certainly hydrated!" He paused. "I eliminated interruptions by skipping social media and emails. I cut the tasks that didn't achieve my most important goal—learning how to make money trading stocks. Every morning, I set a timer for 120 minutes. That's the longest a person can focus on one task without a break. Normally 90 minutes is more realistic for people, but I was so determined and passionate that the time just flew by. After two hours of focused learning, I would start to hear my parents getting ready for work. I met them in the kitchen and got some breakfast with them."

Ben sighed and looked into the distance. "I can still taste my mom's pancakes. Usually burnt!" He looked me up and down, taking in my smart suit. "While studying, I came across several studies that show a direct correlation between smaller waists and increased memory. When I saw photos of executives, they were in shape. I wanted that image, so I began working out. At first, I pushed myself too hard. I ran at maximum speed, lifted huge weights, and spent two hours at the gym every day. But I soon realized I needed to make it enjoyable. Otherwise, I would never stick to the plan long-term." He took a breath.

After a short pause, Ben continued, "Baseball players don't give it 100% at each practice. They work in a comfortable zone. Save 100% for the rare times they need it. Having fun while you learn and work is the best way to remember information. Also, when you enjoy something, you want to continue the routine." Ben pulled out a water bottle from a leather bag and took a drink.

"When it comes to outfits, appearance matters," he continued. "Supervisors look at sloppy employees as, 'if this is how you handle yourself, how will you handle a team?' Look across the way, near the security guard. You see that guy?" I nodded.

"His suit fit well three years ago. He needs to get it altered or buy a new one." Ben shook his head. "I'll tell you something no other interviewee has told you. You know how they say to dress one or two levels above where you are now or dress for the job you want?" I nodded again.

"A load of horse manure. If you dress too nice, expect teasing. People in the office will make fun of you. The only exception to this rule is when you're presenting or out on a sales call. In those two situations, you need to dress for the part." Ben's head snapped up as a woman wearing a dark-blue business suit walked by. She didn't see us. He followed her with his gaze until she was by the elevators, then turned back towards me.

"This reminds me of a story back at my parents' house. I was already trading stocks and was looking for ways to earn more money so I could invest more. In the backyard, we had this old busted-up above-ground swimming pool. I offered to disassemble it and take it to the curb for $200. I was only working on my stock trading for a couple of hours a day, so I had time. After the sun rose, I started. I would roll up the pieces, tie them with rope, and haul them to the street. On the third day, I was tying the last roll of metal when an older pickup truck rolled up to our house. A well-dressed guy got out and started talking to me. He was very interested in what I was doing, and told me he worked for the trash company."

Ben stretched out his long legs and leaned back. "I was so surprised because he was dressed in a suit like an executive. The pickup truck fit the job but not his clothes. We talked about pickup trucks, and he said he wanted to paint his. I suggested that he should paint it like a vintage Mercedes with black on top and grey on the bottom. He loved the idea. At that moment, the garbage truck pulled up. The guys jumped off the back. They recognized the supervisor, then directed their attention to me. The driver of the trash truck told me they would have to charge extra for getting rid of the pool—it was a lot of extra garbage. 'He paid,' the supervisor chimed in. 'I have the paperwork in my truck.'" Ben paused to give me time to write everything down. "Lucky for me, I saved a few bucks by being nice."

"So, if you could give a young high school graduate, only one piece of advice, what would it be?" I asked.

"Hmm, that's a hard one. I guess I'd have to say: Success comes from habits and hobbies." Ben's elusive comment piqued my interest.

"Great artists, like musicians, take control of their fate," he continued. "They reach their goals by practicing. The greatest achievers stay hyper-focused on what they're doing at the time. They don't multitask, and neither should you. Divide your attention, get an inferior outcome. The top performers set unrealistic goals and strive to meet them. They have a growth mindset and practice what they're good at—violin, basketball, golf. They know the results matter most. To get the best outcomes, concentrate on tasks that need the least effort, and have the greatest outcome. Use your strengths and delegate the parts where you aren't strong." Ben paused like he was trying to remember everything he wanted to say.

"Hobbies unrelated to your job are where your best ideas are born. When you have a creative hobby, you use both sides of your brain. Executives who have hobbies come up with the most brilliant ideas during that time. Often, they include minimal noise, allowing the executives to notice the things around them."

"Funny that you say this, you're not the first person to talk about hobbies," I said. "Guess I should get started on that cooking class!"

"Cooking is a great one. Everyone likes tasty food, so it will help you to relate to all kinds of people," Ben said. He checked his watch and jumped up. "Speaking of good food—I have a lunch date and can't afford to be late. Got to go, but call me if you need anything else."

He patted his hair and strode towards the elevators, where the woman in the dark blue suit stood waiting, smiling up at him.

Ben's action steps

- ✓ Use a pleasurable routine during your prime-time to complete your most crucial work distraction-free.
- ✓ During your morning ritual, set a timer—obsessively focus on essential tasks for 90-120 minutes.
- ✓ Set a lofty, near impossible goal and strive to meet it.
- ✓ Find a reason to meet your goal—a new career, hobby, a second source of income, or health.
- ✓ Seek to gain foundational understanding—groundwork.
- ✓ Only start one ritual at a time.
- ✓ Absorb the industry language. A college degree is less important than your skills.
- ✓ Don't multitask.
- ✓ Focus on results. Concentrate on tasks that require the least effort and give the most significant outcome.
- ✓ Use your strengths and delegate the rest.
- ✓ Safeguard and utilize your hobby time to come up with creative solutions.

- ✓ Find a hobby that will also provide exercise.
- ✓ Keep your weight in control.

Ben's favored three

Choose one thing at a time to develop. Spend two weeks focusing solely on this. Once it has become a habit, you can move on to the next improvement.

Spend 90-120 minutes during your prime-time learning a new skill that will help in your career.

Learn all of the relevant jargon in your niche.
- Follow thought leaders on LinkedIn
- Read industry articles and blog posts
- Find online acronym dictionaries in your field
- Search for the terms on YouTube to make sure you are pronouncing them correctly.

Zach used a ball of Play-Doh to double the company's profits

"So you asked how I jumped from a junior executive up two levels within six months?"

Zack walked towards me in the crowded lobby of his gym. He wiped his forehead with a towel and plopped down on one of the oddly shaped plastic chairs.

"Great spin class," he said, as he motioned back toward the studio. I glanced around the lobby, taking in the registration desk, the bright blue lockers, and a small vending machine, where a blonde woman was buying an energy drink.

"Make yourself at home," Zach said and signaled something to a young trainer behind the desk. She brought us some orange drinks I had never tried before. Zack took a deep swig. I stared at my bottle, hesitating as he spoke up again.

"Well, I hired a coach. This girl was the leading expert on executive presence, and I was ready to move up."

I gave him a quizzical look. "But weren't you only in your early twenties?" I asked. "Most people don't hire a coach at that age."

Zach frowned. "You would hire a tutor for your kid. Why not a coach to help you break through a plateau? People hire personal trainers. I hired someone to get me to the next level. After six meetings, I had the promotion."

Zach took another swig of his orange drink and dabbed at his forehead again. Maybe I should give the bottle a go. But it was so . . . orange.

"I wasn't making a ton of money, so I could only afford one meeting per month with her," Zach said. "But that gave me a chance to apply what I learned. The first piece of advice she gave me was to keep presentations between 15 - 20 minutes. The second was to use photos or illustrations during the talks. I did just that. I had to present a good bit, and each time, I kept it under 20 minutes and always used visual aids. Those two elements kept the attention of the people in the meetings, and they remembered what I said. I started to have fun with my presentations, and it showed."

Zach chuckled. "One day, I had a meeting with the top seven executives in the organization. I practiced my presentation at least twenty times. All-in it was 17 minutes." He paused and waited until I finished taking notes.

"I gave a small tub of Play-Doh to each member at the meeting," Zach continued. "I had one too. They kept their hands busy and their focus on me as they messed around with the Play-Doh. My illustrations clearly showed how our top products created much more revenue than the rest of our lineup. I encouraged them to move our focus onto doubling the sales of these top three products and outlined a sales strategy and training for our salespeople. I explained the sales demographics of these products. Then I used a visual to show how we would focus on advertisements geared toward our main customers and talked about specific wording to improve customer service. I finished by taking my Play-Doh, rolling it up into a ball, and showing it to the executives. 'This is where we are today,' I said. Then from under the table, I pulled out a basketball covered in a thin layer of Play-Doh. It looked like it was all made of Play-Doh. I put the two next to one another and told them, 'this is where we're going.'"

Zach smiled. He finished his drink and tossed the empty bottle. "Within six months, my idea was working, and I had a promotion."

"That was fast," I said, flipping a page in my leather-bound book. I picked up my bottle and opened it. 'I'll just go for it,' I thought, closed my eyes and took a swig.

"Wow. Odd shaped bottle and delicious." I smiled at Zach.

"Of course. Do you think I'd buy you something gross?"

He laughed. "Anyway. That coach was worth the money. She made me realize that focusing on the top products was the way forward. 'Sell more of these products—focus on training and sales encouragement, as well as finding the demographics that will buy these products,' she told me. 'Double the sales of the products that bring in the most money.' That is what I spearheaded at my company, and my contribution didn't go unnoticed." Zach paused.

I didn't interrupt. It looked like Zach was thinking. "The coach helped me to draw my focus away from myself and onto the customer. Providing great customer service and terrific customer experience can allow you to sell at a higher price. To be treated well, people will drive further. Customers will wait longer for delivery if they know they'll enjoy the experience."

Zach stopped, walked over to a corner, and pulled out a three-legged stool. "This stool is like customer experience. If it only had two legs, it would fall over. Each leg is important." He touched the first leg. "This one represents connection—every employee who interacts with the customer needs to build a connection." He pointed to the second leg. "This is care—the employees need to put care into the product and customer interactions." He turned the stool around and held onto the final leg. "And this one is a personal concern—show the customer they are important to you."

I took a final swig of my orange drink as Zach stood up.

"Well, I've got to run, but I hope some of this helps," he said. "Feel free to stay. They've got green, blue, and purple drinks as well." With a wink, he sauntered out of the building.

Zach's action steps

- ✓ Keep your presentation 15-20 minutes long and incorporate photos or illustrations.
- ✓ Focus most of your efforts on the products that generate the most profits to double sales.
- ✓ Provide excellent customer service and experience.

The top three from Zach

When you prepare your next presentation, follow these two rules:
- ☙ Length: 15-20 minutes.
- ☙ Use photos and illustrations.

Analyze all of your products and choose your 2 - 3 bestsellers.

- How can I sell more of these products?
- How can the customer experience be enriched when selling these products?
- Who is the target demographic, and what are they looking for?

Take a sheet of paper and write three columns: Connection - Care - Concern.

- Find three examples of how you and your employees have demonstrated these values to your customers in the past.
- Find three possibilities of how you and your employees can improve in each area.

The advice Phyllis got was worth billions to the company and promotions for her

"Your handwritten letter was a nice touch." Phyllis pointed to a wing-back armchair, inviting me to sit. I thought it odd to have such a beautiful chair in a busy hotel. I sank into its folds and almost vanished in the ample stuffing, then looked at Phyllis. She was not a woman to cross. With her hair drawn back into a tight bun and her high-necked dress, she looked strict and efficient: every inch the CEO of a prominent English firm.

"Can I get you started on some tea and scones?" My head snapped around, and I stared at the waiter in a smart tuxedo, holding a polished silver tray. He must have approached in complete silence.

"Yes, please, and I ordered the vegetarian option," Phyllis replied. Her accent was less polished than the waiters, but you could hear the English influence.

'Living here for fifteen years, I suppose you adapt,' I thought and let my gaze sweep past the ornate decorations of the Savoy Hotel and onto the street beyond. A black London taxi cab was dropping off some hotel guests, and I suddenly wished that I, too, was staying in the luxurious Savoy. I turned my head back to the waiter, but he had vanished as silently as he'd arrived.

Phyllis looked at me. "College didn't teach me what got me to the top. I learned it from a life-coach. I'm not saying it will take you 20 minutes to put-in-place what I learned, but I'll give you the same advice she gave me. This lady charged $3,900 for ten hours of her time, which seemed like a staggering amount back then." She paused. "In all honesty, that $3,900 has more than paid for itself. Look where I'm sitting." She gestured at the sparkling plates and silverware, then gazed up at the ornate ceiling.

"If you want your company to have triple-digit growth, focus on customer service and customer experience," she continued.

I made some notes, then looked up as I waited for Phyllis to continue.

"Customer service is reactive. The situation is the problem, not the customer. Our agents make certain the customer knows their problem matters and that we are personally concerned about it. Each agent will start by paraphrasing the grievance, then say a few words to show he or she cares. We then ask the person what we can do to keep them as a customer. Our agents are empowered problem solvers. They'll propose a generous fix without management approval." She stopped talking and sat quietly.

I was about to say something when Phyllis continued, "On the other hand, customer experience is proactive. It's how our company makes the client feel. Do the service and product exceed their expectations?" She paused.

"We are trying to get the customer to be our promoters by giving them the best possible experience. We want them to have an emotional attachment to our company. Today's marketing is all about customer reviews—star ratings" Phyllis stared at me in silence.

"That's . . ." I tried to interject.

"Customer experience comes down to focus," Phyllis interrupted me. "We don't focus on what we do, but rather on how we do it. Waitrose doesn't just sell groceries—they focus on the customer experience. As soon as you step into a shop, you can feel the care that has been put into arranging products to make your visit more convenient. Same with their website: tailored shopping, easy importing of lists, and an online 'trolley.' All to make the customer's weekly shop as easy as possible."

She paused as I thought back to my first Waitrose visit the day before and how the assistant had taken me right to the product I needed. It was true. The English upmarket shop was a master at creating a positive experience.

"To have great customer experience, the clients need to think of your company and say to themselves, 'They made me feel cared for,'" Phyllis continued. "It's about making customers feel special—spoil them like a VIP. What's the cost of a faultless website? It's nothing for you but makes the client feel your extraordinary care. There are a few other ways to make clients feel exceptional. You can use fun-loving, low-cost favors such as a free refill. Rearrange your schedule to accommodate their needs. Give them a follow-up phone call. Another one is to give your customer the direct line to someone high up in the company."

The waiter returned with a tray laden with steaming tea and treats in pastel colors, most of which I couldn't name. Phyllis thanked him and took a sip of her herbal tea, then sat back in her chair.

"When I first came to this company, I took the advice of that high-paid life-coach," Phyllis said. "That advice prompted me to change the company's language for success. The coach gave me examples, and the one that stuck out to me was Disney. They don't call all those people a crowd; they use 'audience.' Employees are 'cast members.' Customers are 'guests.'" She paused and cut up a tiny macaroon, then popped a piece into her mouth.

She chewed and continued, "We made a lot of changes. We've eliminated small things, like those common signs in the bathrooms. Instead of 'Employees must wash hands,' ours now read, 'We value cleanliness and always wash our hands before returning to work.' Instead of making clients verify it's them, we update their information. We, like other companies, have a 'never' and 'always' list for employees to follow." Phyllis pulled a piece of paper out of her handbag and handed it to me:

Never	Always
Point.	Lead.
Say 'No.'	Find a solution.
Say 'I don't know.'	Say 'Let me find out.'
Say 'No problem.'	Say 'My pleasure.'
Say 'It's our policy.'	Say 'Here's how I can help you.'
Show frustration.	Be friendly.

"Impressive," I said.

Phyllis smiled and nodded. "Make your contracts as simple as possible. Customers don't like 'gotcha clauses' in the contract. If we used a trick like that to get more money, the client would talk poorly about us. We want them to know we care about them, and if they aren't happy, we'll make it right, or they can get out of the contract." She stopped and dabbed her mouth with the white napkin.

"So now you know how I rose to the top. I stood on two pillars: customer service and customer experience. I put those at the forefront for this company, and the top executives liked what I was saying and kept promoting me. As far as the $3,900, it was money well spent. The advice I got has made the company number one in its market, creating billions of dollars of revenue. Not a bad ROI."

She put down the napkin, and the waiter appeared immediately.
"Sir, madam, are you finished with the tea?" He asked. "I trust everything was to your satisfaction?"

"It was great," I spoke up, slightly embarrassed at my coarse American twang.

"Excellent, thank you," Phyllis said. She took out her credit card and handed it to him. Within two minutes, he was back with the receipt. I glanced at it and had to hold in a gasp. £150 for two teas and a few cakes! They were delicious, but I could still feel my stomach rumbling.

'Guess money is not an issue for Phyllis,' I thought. 'I'm going out for a Chicago-style pizza tonight.'

Phyllis' action steps

- ✓ Focus on customer service and customer experience.
- ✓ Ask the client what their problem is. The client's problem is your priority.
- ✓ Paraphrase their grievance.
- ✓ Talk straight from the gut to show you genuinely care.
- ✓ Ask what you can do.
- ✓ Empower employee problem solvers by giving them the authority to make decisions.
- ✓ Propose a generous fix.
- ✓ Focus on having the client feel expectations are exceeded.
- ✓ Make customers feel special and cared for.
- ✓ Use fun-loving, low-cost, favors.
- ✓ Change the language for success.
- ✓ Update your Never and Always lists to match trends.
- ✓ Eliminate small print clauses.

The top three Phyllis would recommend following

Evaluate your customer service. On a 1-10 scale, how is the following?

- ଔ Make it easy for the customer to contact you.
- ଔ Paraphrase the customer's problem.
- ଔ Say or write a few words to show you care.
- ଔ Ask the customer what you can do to keep them.
- ଔ If any areas scored below an 8, work to fix it.

> Pro Tip: Remove the number 7 from your scale. 7 is a safe option - not too bad, not too good. If you don't include it, your evaluation will be much more precise.

Alter the language you use to reflect the values of your company

Create a 'Never' and 'Always' list for yourself. What are phrases you never want to say, and how can you replace them with something more productive?
- Once you have a short list, share it with your employees, and make it company policy.

Chuck Norris started a fire in a classroom, and it lit Lou ablaze

"I was in high school," Lou said as we sat down at a lovely restaurant in New York City called Eleven Madison Park. Our round table was a few steps higher than the main dining area, and I looked over at the other guests, most of whom were business people out for lunch. I sat back in my mocha-colored suede chair and placed my hands on the pristine white linen. "Anything to drink?" A waiter asked.

I scanned the menu, inhaling sharply at the prices.

"Just water for me, thanks," I mumbled.

Lou waved his hand and said," Two Gran Mayan Ultra Aged Añejos, neat please." With a wink, he turned back towards me. "If you don't like the tequila, it won't go to waste. As I was saying, I moved to this new town right at the start of high school. First thing on Monday morning, I walked into Dave Norris' Chemistry class. It was a small town—everyone knew each other, so the students glanced at me curiously. From the back row, one student started to chant, 'Fire Chuck, fire! Fire Chuck FIRE!' The entire class joined in. I didn't know this back then, but all the students called this teacher, Chuck. He in no way resembled Chuck Norris, but he never minded the nickname. I think he secretly started it." Lou smiled. At that moment, the drinks arrived, sparkling from the sun pouring through the large windows.

"Any appetizers?" The waiter asked.

I frowned at the menu again. "Uhh . . ."

"Two, please. Beluga caviar," Lou said. I raised my eyebrows but didn't comment. Surely, he wouldn't ask me to pay.

"Back to high school. Chuck pulled out two bottles as students moved the tables out of the way," Lou continued. "He squirted the liquids onto the tile floor in cursive writing. I strained to see what it said, but another student pulled me back. 'Careful,' he whispered. Suddenly, the floor was ablaze with a raging fire. The flames in the middle of the classroom spelled out, 'Welcome, Lou.'" He paused and took a sip of the tequila. "Chuck taught me something about leadership that day. A leader has to have the skill—they have to be able to get the job done."

The waiter arrived with a tiny plate of appetizers. 'These can't be worth the price,' I thought. But one bite of that beluga caviar taught me otherwise. It tasted like ambrosia. Lou smacked his lips and chewed for a few minutes before continuing. "Chuck taught me a lot about leadership in less than a year. He taught me that a leader has to have the right attitude, be able to manage stress, and know who to avoid in your life." Lou ate a bit more of his caviar.

After Lou dabbed his mouth with the white napkin, he continued, "We were talking about who to avoid. The class had these baby chickens. We raised them from eggs. One day Chuck was running late, and a student named Doug took one of the baby chicks and put it in the desk. You know, the type of desk with the opening in the front. We could hear it chirping and looked at each other uneasily as Chuck walked in. He saw our faces and ran over to the chicks. He noticed one was missing. Knowing instinctively what had happened, Chuck went over to Doug and demanded, 'Give me that chick back!' Doug shook his head. Chuck grabbed the back of Doug's chair and said, 'I know you have that baby chick. Give it back!' Chuck pulled Doug's seat backward. What no one knew was Doug had a Bic lighter in the desk, and the evil student was letting all the gas escape. Before Chuck yanked Doug away, he lit it on fire. An explosion and a burnt chick burst from the desk. The student was expelled. Some people are evil; don't deal with them. Get them out of your life."

The waiter came to take our main dinner order.

"Poached lobster with butternut squash," Lou said.

I shrugged my shoulders. "Who doesn't like lobster as they overlook Madison Park in New York? I'll have the same."

Lou asked the waiter for two Bénédictines neat, then turned back towards me. "Vision cast every 42 days. Tell your employees where the company is going and how they'll get there every six weeks. They need renewed focus, and you are the driving force." The drinks arrived, and I knocked mine back. The room spun slightly, and I grinned at Lou.

"When I went to college, I had a great professor called Clarence White. He always said, 'It costs you nothing but time to stop what you're doing and pay attention to people.' He taught us to listen to them. Give your undivided attention." Lou paused to finish his Bénédictine.

"I used to take care of Dr. White's dogs while he went away. I guess I was one of his favorite students. It helped me out, I got away from my roommates for a long weekend, and he had a hot tub. Whenever I needed to talk with Dr. White, he stopped what he was doing. He pushed his keyboard and mouse away, slid his chair to the left, and faced me. He gave me his undivided attention, even when he was busy." Lou stopped again and grinned. "Those were the days. I had so much fun with his dogs. We taught one of them to say, 'I love you.' Granted it sounded like a dog howl, but you could hear 'I wuv youuu.'"

We chuckled, and at that moment, our main course arrived.

"Thank you. The squash smells fantastic," Lou said. We took a few bites, then Lou looked up, gesturing around the dining hall.

"It was here at this restaurant years ago that I met the CEO of a Fortune 500 company. I was a kid, and I had only recently graduated from college. That summer, I interned at this mega-corporation. Susan, my direct supervisor, who was a big-wig herself, told me to take a walk with her. We came to the revolving doors of this restaurant and outside was the CEO of our company. She introduced me and then told me to meet her back at the office. The CEO stopped her and insisted I eat lunch with them. I learned a lesson from that CEO: be nice to everyone—build relationships. You never know where people will end up."

He paused to take another bite of his lobster. "As we ate lunch that Friday afternoon, the CEO made Susan feel valued. He kept telling her how she was a producer—could get the job done. Then, he confided in both of us he wanted to take-over a rival company. This guy was trusting inside information in front of me, a kid who graduated from college a few months ago. I saw first-hand that leaders need to trust the people working with them and show them that trust. The CEO wasn't about following rules. He was about building relationships. Susan was the one who was going to head up the acquisition." Lou paused to finish the last few bites of lobster, then set his knife and fork diagonally on the plate to signal the end of the meal.

"You know how some leaders are like, 'It's my way or the highway sucker!' Well, not this guy. He included me, set aside his ambition, and showed trust. Employees follow supervisors who are stronger than themselves. This guy was more durable than the Hulk." The waiter came and took Lou's plate as well as mine, then handed us the dessert menu.

I didn't think twice this time. "The milk and honey custard with bee pollen ice cream, please."

"Good selection," Lou said and ordered a cheese fondue.

"People follow leaders who have done something special for them—personally," Lou said. "Special attention increases performance. When you invest in people, you deepen your relationships—strengthening loyalty and increasing performance. When my internship with Susan ended, I went to her to thank her for the great experience. I knew she was busy, but like Dr. White, she pushed everything to the side to talk with me. She must have spent three hours talking. In the end, she set up an interview for me as a junior executive. I got the job, and 90% of the reason was Susan's recommendation. Just like her CEO, Susan taught me that you earn trust when you show people you enjoy their contributions and treat them as individuals with values and unique talents. Treating people this way is how to build a loyal team and become a true leader." The waiter brought the bill, and Lou paid.

We walked through the revolving door and stood on the sidewalk. "You won't find EP-101 as a college class," Lou said. "You also won't reach a high level of leadership with merely a degree. But both EP and leadership are taught. You can read about them or learn from people who have been there. But it's up to you to pull the pearls out of the oysters to make your necklace."

With a nod and a smile, he walked away.

Lou's action steps

- ✓ Spend time on developing your skills to get the job done.
- ✓ Learn how to deal with pressure, failure, deadlines, and obstacles.
- ✓ Remain positive during bad times.
- ✓ Vision cast every six weeks.
- ✓ Give your undivided attention to your clients, coworkers, and projects.
- ✓ Build relationships and be kind to everyone.
- ✓ Value each person—communicate how you feel about individual team members.
- ✓ Trust and confide in the people working with you.
- ✓ Prioritize relationships over rules.
- ✓ Refine your table manners and etiquette.
- ✓ Present yourself as reliable and approachable. People will only follow leaders stronger than them.
- ✓ To improve performance, do individual and specific things for your teammates.
- ✓ When you like people, it shows—tell them as an individual how valuable they are, build loyalty, and become the leader.

Lou's top three

Develop your skills.
- Table manners.
- Building relationships.

Focus on the person who wants to talk with you.
- The next time an employee approaches you or asks to speak to you, give your full attention, and take the time to listen. Observe how your relationship with the employee changes.

Trust your employees.
- Speak to your employees about plans related to your firm. Include them in the ideas by asking for their input and help.

References

Weil, D. A. (2020, 6 2). *Healing Benefits*. Retrieved from 478 Breathing Exercises: https://healingbenefits.blogspot.com/2012/09/478-breathing-exercises.html

Winfrey, O. (2020, 6 2). *Oprah.com*. Retrieved from Every Person Has a Purpose: https://www.oprah.com/spirit/how-oprah-winfrey-found-her-purpose

www.ingramcontent.com/pod-product-compliance
Lightning Source LLC
Chambersburg PA
CBHW060431220526
45465CB00008B/3091